Heroes I've Known

George Holt Jr.

ISBN- 978-0-578-67832-0

TABLE OF CONTENTS

PART 1. GEORGE T. MACDONALD

Chapter One - Bayonets Fixed   *9*
Chapter Two - The Pleasant Life   *11*
Chapter Three - Escape and Evade   *15*
Chapter Four – Capture   *24*
Chapter Five - Off to Prison?   *27*
Chapter Six - Bound for Los Baños   *31*
Chapter Seven - Daily Life at Los Baños   *36*
Chapter Eight - Vanderpool and the Guerrillas   *51*
Chapter Nine - Concern for the POWs   *57*
Chapter Ten - MacArthur Returns   *63*
Chapter Eleven – Starvation   *69*
Chapter Twelve - Planning the Rescue   *74*
Chapter Thirteen - Airborne Assault Planning   *82*
Chapter Fourteen - The Raid &Rescue   *86*
Epilogue   *102*
Research Notes   *107*

PART 2. JAMES "OBIE" OBENAUF

Chapter One - The Mission   *115*
Chapter Two - The Aircraft   *122*
Chapter Three - The Aircrew   *133*
Chapter Four - James "Obie" Obenauf   *136*
Chapter Five - Explosion and Fire   *141*
Chapter Six - Wing Commander Interview   *155*
Chapter Seven - Obie's Awards   *160*
Chapter Eight - Above All Awards   *169*
Chapter Nine - The TV Star   *172*
Chapter Ten - Obie the B-58 Driver   *175*
Chapter Eleven - Obie in retirement   *178*
Research Notes   *183*

ABOUT THE AUTHOR   *185*
APPENDIX A - Babies born in Los Baños Camp   *187*
APPENDIX B - Marriages in Los Baños Camp   *188*
APPENDIX C - Roster of 11 Navy Nurses   *188*
APPENDIX D - LOS BAÑOS INTERNEES   *189*

Acknowledgements

I would like to acknowledge the contributions made by Lt. Colonel James E. Obenauf and Lt. Colonel George T. MacDonald during the writing of this book. They first provided valuable historical and personal background material. Then they reviewed a number of drafts, and made significant comments, to ensure the accuracy of the heroic events portrayed in their lives.

Also, I'd like to thank the edits and recommendations provided by my two sisters Doris Hutchins and Elizabeth Palm. As in other books I've authored, they have never hesitated to step forward to provide their support.

Thanks to Colonel George Alan Dugard an author in his own right, who provided valuable suggestions for rearranging certain text in the book for a better chronological flow of events.

Finally, to my wife Deb Holt, a special thanks for all of the helpful edits that have made this book just that much better.

Foreword

This book is about the bravery displayed by two men I've known, Lt. Colonel George MacDonald and Lt. Colonel James Obenauf.

It is a two part story – really two books in one.

The first part is the story of a brave young eleven year old lad who was captured by the Japanese and how he and his family managed to survive 3 years in captivity. As prisoners of war in the Philippines, they faced severe starvation and were threatened with mass extermination when the Japanese began losing the war in 1945.

The second story is about a young Air Force copilot who had to make a life threatening decision. The pilot and navigator had bailed out of a bomber aircraft after an engine exploded. The copilot's ejection seat failed to work. He had the choice to leave the aircraft through the navigator's open hatch or try to save the life of another officer on board who had been knocked unconscious. You'll see if he made the right decision.

I served with both of these gentlemen when all three of us flew in the supersonic B-58 bomber. George and James were pilots. I was a navigator/bombardier. I am proud to call them my friends.

George Holt Jr.
Author

George Holt, Jr.

Heroes I've Known

Part 1.

George T. MacDonald

11 Year Old Prisoner of War

George Holt, Jr.

Chapter One

Bayonets Fixed

George was 11 years old when the United States entered World War II, after the Japanese bombed Pearl Harbor on December 7th 1941. He and his parents, Presbyterian missionaries, were living in the Philippine Islands. When the Japanese invaded and began occupying the Philippines, many American families hid from the Japanese to avoid capture. [1]

In July 1942, George and his Dad went to get water from a spring and bring it back to a small remote house in the mountains where the family had been hiding from the Japanese. His Dad took a bath in the spring and returned to the house carrying water.

George remained at the spring and recalls, "I was now all alone, taking my bath. I had a large prune can which I used to pour water over me. Just pouring some water over me to rinse myself off, I heard a noise behind me. Turning to see soldiers accompanied by Filipinos, I was petrified, even more so when they withdrew bayonets from their scabbards and fixed them on their rifles! I was in a complete quandary. I'd never seen an enemy soldier before and here they are, fixing their bayonets. Needless to say, there wasn't any doubt in my mind that they were Japanese.' [2]

"I raised my hands for want of a better thing to do, and the can slipped from my hand, making a horrible clatter as it struck the

9

rocks. While standing there, petrified and shaking, one of the soldiers grabbed me by the left arm and led me up the hill.'

As an 11 year old American boy, the greatest responsibility George had up until this time was to do his homework, get good grades in school and of course try to stay out of trouble. Then the war started and he really had no comprehension of what that meant.

This was the day the Japanese captured the MacDonald family and for the next three years they would lose their freedom, face starvation, and eventually be threatened with extermination.

Before the war started, there were eight in the MacDonald family. Two of the six children, were in the United States. One was going to college and another to nursing school. George's older brother Robert was living in Manila attending high school and living with another missionary family. His next older brother John and sister Helen lived with George and his parents in the town of Legaspi, in the Philippines. Legaspi is where George was born.

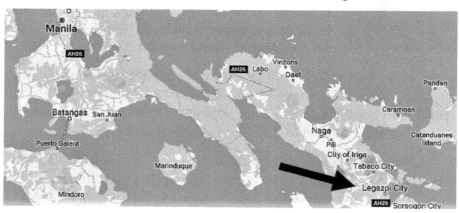

George's father went to the Philippines in 1909 followed by his wife Margaret in 1922. After being assigned to the town of Legaspi, his father covered the entire area by preaching and teaching. He was also instrumental in establishing a mission bible school which had resident students attend from all over the area.

Chapter Two

The Pleasant Life

Life was pleasant for them in Legaspi. Kenneth MacDonald kept occupied with his missionary work and wife Margaret kept busy with the family and her many piano students.

Mission kids 1933, George is on the wagon in the middle.

What a wonderful family they raised as can be seen from the following photographs.

1936, Kenneth, Bob, Sibyl, George, Janet, John, Helen and Margaret.

John, Helen and George off to school 1939

Then in 1941 everything changed.

George's Dad kept a comprehensive diary while in the Philippines. One of his entries before the war started, reads,

"In October or November of 1941, orders came out from Washington to send back to the States all army, navy and air force wives and children. Naturally all U.S. civilians like us began to take notice but all inquiries were answered with the assurance that 'nothing was going to happen.' In spite of these repeated assurances, the idea that war might not come, was hard to swallow.'

There were some who gave Japan credit for having too much sense to get involved in a war with the United States. However, Kenneth MacDonald was seeing increasing evidence that something dire was about to happen, as seen in this diary entry.

"Friday evening, Dec. 5th, we went to the Railroad Station to pick up Dr. and Mrs. Tom Cook, missionaries from Korea who had been driven out by the Japanese. They came to the Philippines to relieve us, the MacDonalds, who were to go on a one year furlough in the States, starting in April. To our surprise we found the whole area around the station packed with Filipino soldiers being returned to the Manila area. HA! if war did come it began to look as if we would be left strictly on our own. Our apprehension began to grow.'

"Monday morning broke bright and fair. As usual I got downstairs just in time to turn on the radio for the 6:30 broadcast. The first thing I heard was a blast that nearly floored me! 'The Japanese have bombed Pearl Harbor and destroyed much of the pacific fleet.' The radio was never turned off all day. We hung on it for details. They came aplenty but were often conflicting.'

"Later in the day came the news that Aparri and Davao had been bombed. (the most northern and southern towns in the Philippines) Clearly, we were in a war and there were no protecting forces anywhere near, but it could not last more than a month or two! Just a case of waiting it out till our forces could arrive from the States!'

13

"Naturally shipping would be disrupted so we laid in a stock of rice, canned milk, beans, and canned meats. It also occurred to me that there might be a run on the local bank and it would have to close, so I drew out 600 pesos ($300) in small bills and silver and put it in my office safe. We decided our most probable danger would be from bombing and our good concrete houses would doubtless make nice targets."

George and his Dad looked for a good place to stay in case the family had to leave in a hurry. They were successful in finding a shelter in the little barrio of Malobago. It was a location where his Dad had held church services on selected Sundays.

The author notes that when war began in the Pacific, Japan had two major goals: a surprise attack on Pearl Harbor at the outset of the war; and the Southern Operation, aimed at capturing the Philippines, Malaya, and the Dutch East Indies. [3]

Admiral Yamamoto was a brilliant tactician who planned and carried out the successful attack on Pearl Harbor, but as a strategist he was an utter failure, because that attack awakened a sleeping giant–the United States.

The family's move to Malobago came sooner than expected.

Chapter Three

Escape and Evade

The family was asleep on the morning of December 12th. At 5:00 AM, Dr. and Mrs. Cook woke them up. They said, "The Japanese are landing on the seashore, we should leave."

While packing clothes, a Filipino friend came and said, "The Japanese are coming up the road from Legaspi. Hurry or you'll be trapped."

"Dad hollered to my mother, 'Get everyone in the car. Come around the house and I'll jump on the running board!' He had to go by the office and pick up the money he had withdrawn from the bank."

Now with money in hand, they reached the main road, and not seeing any Japanese in sight, they decided to head out for Malobago to sit it out and assess the situation from there.

"There were eight in the car: my parents, us kids, Dr. and Mrs. Cook and Dave Martin, a missionary from Japan. Dave had decided to come to the Philippines to help our mission while he sent his family back to the United States. This turned out to be a blessing in disguise, as Dave was fluent in Japanese and served as our interpreter for most of the war."

Olive Rohrbaugh, a single missionary in her sixties, drove her own car and came later in the day, bringing three children belonging

15

to Dr. and Mrs. McAnlis. Dr. William McAnlis was the mission doctor in Legaspi. He and his wife Jo stayed behind at the mission hospital, hoping they could keep working.

In Malobago they had just a small building that had been used for church services on Sundays, kind of isolated but still it was on one of the main roads through the area. This made it difficult to stay hidden. Not that the Filipinos were going to tell on them but the villagers couldn't help but talk amongst themselves about the Americans they had seen.

"While at Malobago, we went to some high ground and watched airplanes in the distance, always hoping they were our planes, but they were not because bombing was taking place."

Magon 火山「レガスピー」附近 16-12-12

Carrier Attack Bombers flying from aircraft carrier Ryujo are shown flying near Mayon Volcano on their way to attack Legaspi. [38]

It quickly became evident to everyone that they couldn't stay at this place very long. The road was too close, they had to find a more secluded hide out. Days later they found the right place, a native

16

bamboo house, built on stilts, about a half mile away and about 200 yards off the road.

They would be sleeping on the floor as there were no beds available, but mosquito netting, a prized possession, adequately  protected them. Their daily routine included things for the kids to do to keep them occupied and out of mischief. They wove mats and Dr. Cook was an accomplished flautist and he made them flutes out of bamboo. This worked well and the kids were soon learning to play the flutes and were making some pretty good music.

Singing was another pastime.

'America The Beautiful' was George MacDonald's favorite song, and he said, "It still is. It helped to keep our spirits up."

They had many Filipino visitors coming by and bringing them supplies. One of their Filipino doctors brought needed medical supplies. However, it soon became evident that even being 200 yards off the road, it was still not safe, so numerous trips were taken to checkout better locations further inland. Christmas and New Year's celebrations at Malobago were spent quite differently than in years past.

Jo McAnlis, the Doctor's wife, decided to join her children and reached Malobago on the 3rd of January, with the help of Filipino friends. The trip took three weeks, much of the time by foot, sometimes by carabao (water buffalo) and once in a bold ride by car.

Having to go through a checkpoint, a Filipino had her lie on the floorboard of his car and covered her with very dusty, course cloth abaca sacks. For a woman who was allergic even to face powder, she miraculously made it without sneezing. Jo was quite travel-worn by the time she arrived, but was so happy to see her children. Unfortunately, Dr. McAnlis was subsequently taken prisoner by the Japanese.

There was always this constant fear that they would be captured and soon after Jo McAnlis' arrival they got word from friends that the Japanese were interested in them. Whether or not they had been betrayed, they didn't know, but the situation got tense.

Some Filipinos were sympathetic to the Japanese cause. In fact, towards the end of the war the Japanese gave them official recognition, calling them 'Makapili'. They turned in many Filipinos suspected of being guerrillas.

The decision was made to move again, and about midnight, with Filipinos to help carry their belongings, they started the three mile hike across the mountains of Albay. "Our oldest missionary, Olive Rohrbaugh, rode a carabao part of the way. Being in her 60's she was not able to hike across the mountains, especially at night."

The trek took about four hours to the barrio of Palanas. School was not in session so they made arrangements to stay in the school house, shown here.

"We enjoyed it for the time we were there. A nearby river allowed us to go swimming almost every day. We were without running water, bathrooms and showers at Malobago, so this was a special treat."

However, it was right on one of the main trails through the hills and very visible. Knowing they could not stay there for a protracted period; they started a search for a place less visible. They found a more remote place in the small village of Lilibdon about 2 miles away.

It was off the main route through the mountains, but it was small and their group had become larger—thirteen people in all. At least one large room would have to be added to double the space. For now this place was at the top of their list in case they had to move again.

They had been at Palanas about 10 days, when one afternoon one of their Filipino Christians came with a warning that four Japanese and two Filipinos had been looking for them and now were on their way to Palanas.

A little later another friend came with the same warning. They had just sat down for dinner and while praying before eating, two more Filipinos came bursting in with word that the Japanese were only about three miles away. It was definitely time to leave for Lilibdon.

"Talk about the Israelites picking up and running, we packed up our necessary stuff and got underway inside of fifteen minutes. Unfortunately, we had to leave our dinner on the stove."

It was quite dark with only a sliver of a moon showing as they made their way silently, single file up the path to Lilibdon and it seemed to take forever.

The owner was surprised at their arrival, but graciously packed up all the things from his house and moved in on his relatives. They slept on the bamboo floor that night with the mosquito nets, and the next morning they decided it wasn't too bad.

A typical house in this part of the country.

The following map shows the route the family took over those many days from their home in Legaspi to Malobago, Palanas and finally Lilibdon.

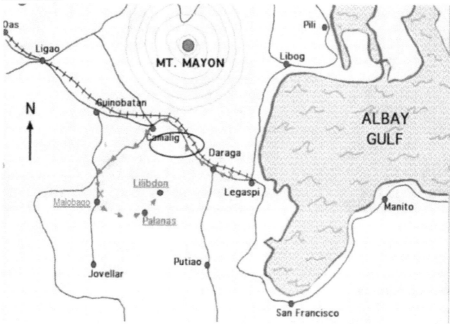

At Lilibdon, because of the house's small size and because they knew they were being pursued by the Japanese, they set up their baggage so they could pick up and depart on a moment's notice. Their house was at the top of a small hill and had a lean-to out back for cooking. At the base of the hill was a small clearing with a fresh water spring. A rock catch-basin that provided an excellent water source.

George's parents, Kenneth and Margaret MacDonald are shown here in 1941 with John 13, Helen 15 and George, far right at 11.

Filipino friends notified them about their home town of Legaspi. The Japanese had substantially reduced their presence there to a small occupation force and there were no ships nor airplanes. So, because of that good news, they decided that Lilibdon would be their final hide-away location. "With thirteen people in our group, youngsters, middle age, and older people, it would not be easy to evade the Japanese. For that reason we decided to stay put, make ourselves as comfortable as possible, and see if we could ride out the war there."

"Everybody was assigned a job around the camp. Dad did a lot of the construction and built a Dutch oven for baking bread. He and I were responsible for carrying the water from the spring and filling the stone jars up at the house.'

"We had two Filipina young ladies from the Visayan Islands, students at their Bible school, who did the cooking for the group in return for a place to sleep and food to eat. They did an excellent job of cooking, despite the size of our group."

21

People got sick off and on with dengue fever, a mosquito-borne disease causing flu-like symptoms. They would get piercing headaches, muscle and joint pains, fever and full body rashes. They all had spells of illness due to the warm, rainy weather, but managed to survive. George remembers his brother John helping his Dad improve the area of the spring and how John ended up hitting his toe with a crow bar resulting in a long period of sickness.

Church services were held every Sunday and local Filipinos were invited, but this, in the long run, contributed to the MacDonald's and the others' undoing. People talk. People listen. Rumors spread and all it takes is just one Japanese sympathizer to turn them in.

There wasn't a lot of reading material, no radio, nor newspapers so they had to keep occupied. The garden was something which everyone helped weed and water. They'd get plenty of food from the vendors who came by or they'd get permission to go out and harvest their own, such as bananas. Rope was made using hemp processed from abaca trees, the same species as banana trees.

Lilibdon in summer of 1942. George and his mother are far left in this photo.

They kept busy, but were always anxious to get news of the war, good or bad. It was usually bad. Even in 1942 they'd get rumors of American troops on the way which always turned out to be false.

Chapter Four

Capture

July 2nd 1942:

Thus far, the MacDonalds and their friends had been able to escape and evade the Japanese for six months. Quite a feat, however it must have been quite sad for the McAnlis family, especially the children who had not seen their father for over six months. And then like a miracle, who should arrive on this day but Dr. McAnlis.

He had been taken prisoner and interned in the town of Naga. Filipino guerrillas then raided the town and set him and other prisoners free. When Filipino Christians heard of the rescue, they contacted and hid him. Through the grapevine he found out where the MacDonalds were and after a hard trek, he walked into their encampment at Lilibdon.

His arrival was ill-fated because their capture by the Japanese came within two weeks after his arrival.

That was the morning when George was captured while bathing in the spring.

As Japanese soldiers led George back to the house, he was herded into a group outside. One of the soldiers saw that he was wet and suggested that he go in the house and get on something dry.

"My mother, when she heard that, leaned over and whispered to me, 'Get my watch. It's hanging on the post in our room.' I was then escorted into the house, changed my clothes, got her watch, and returned to stand with our group.'

Dave Martin was speaking in Japanese to the soldier-in-charge when he was slapped very hard. "I had never seen a person slapped like that before, but whatever he was trying to tell him, the soldier didn't like it.'

"They told us to pack up, that we were returning to Legaspi. We started out with everyone carrying something, but with only a small amount of our possessions. We walked on this trail for what was to be about a two mile hike.'

After about half an hour, the procession stopped. Three soldiers set up their mortar and fired two or three rounds up on top of an adjacent hill, apparently thinking that they had seen Filipino guerrillas.

They continued to a village where their Filipino guide who was leading the group was paid for his services by the Japanese. Later they found out that Filipino guerrillas had killed him that very night.

In most cases it didn't pay to inform on Americans, since most Filipinos were still loyal to the cause. The 'cause' being the eventual independence of the Philippines from being a U.S. protectorate to becoming a fully independent nation. The U.S. fully supported that transition. Of course, the war interrupted the process.

The group had to wait on the road for quite a while for transportation. A bus finally arrived and took them to Legaspi, back to their old stomping grounds.

They moved into a house that used to belong to friends of theirs. It was a typical tropical house made out of wood, a galvanized iron roof, lots of porches, some screening, but open so the trade winds could come through and provide ventilation. It was a fairly good size house and provided adequate shelter for their group, now a total of 17 people.

Two guards were stationed there, one in front and one in back of the house, but they weren't too worried about anyone escaping, because as George said, "I can recall a time when a soldier disassembled his rifle, cleaned it and put it back together again while on guard duty."

The Japanese were friendly in the beginning, and the group were fed quite well, but some labor was required of them. The adults went out and cleaned up the area, cutting grass, and getting things back in shape.

"Strangely enough, we could not see our old house from our new location, but we did see several of our old Filipino classmates from school, although we couldn't talk to them. We saw a pack of dogs go by the first day and thought we saw our dog, Brownie, but weren't really sure. We kept an eye out for the dogs and the next time they came by we identified Brownie and called him and he came to us. He was very happy to see us and stayed with us while we lived there."

At times they experienced acts of kindness. The Japanese officer-in-charge came in many times to see if they were comfortable and had everything they needed. Once when the kids were playing on the porch, he asked them if they liked to play dominoes.

"We said sure, then he left. That evening after we had gone to bed, we heard this thump, thump, thump, up the steps, onto the porch and here he came into the house, hunted us up and said, 'Here are your dominoes.' That was one act of kindness."

Chapter Five

Off to Prison?

After three weeks in Legaspi the group was abruptly told that they would be leaving and to be ready at five the next morning.

After fitful spurts of sleep, they were awakened at three, told to pack and were then ready to leave at five. They were bussed to the port of Legaspi, boarded a Japanese freighter and with the sun coming up they sailed out of Albay Gulf.

Stopping at Aroroy for cargo, they continued on and after three days of sailing they entered Manila Bay and docked at the port. From there they were transported to Santo Tomas Internment Camp where they faced an unsure future. This map shows the boat ride to Manila.

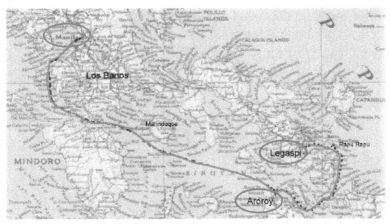

Washing up at Santo Tomas.

After arriving at Santo Tomas, they were somewhat heartened to learn of a Japanese proposal to allow missionaries to be placed in a mission compound in the city of Manila. There they would be allowed to continue their religious activities of teaching and preaching.

"The Japanese had a problem with whether we had surrendered or whether we were captured. It apparently was to make a difference. In any case we remained at Santo Tomas for three weeks before our conditional release finally came through."

They left Santo Tomas and were bussed to the Presbyterian mission compound where they would live under house arrest. They were restricted from traveling anywhere in Manila without a pass. Their release was more a matter of the Japanese not wanting to have to provide food and housing for so many internees.

The missionaries were not allowed to do gainful work, but had to maintain themselves during this time. Many Christian business men advanced them money, knowing they would be reimbursed someday.

This is Ellinwood Church in the Presbyterian Mission Compound. Grace Nash, a friend of George MacDonald and author of the book, 'That We Might Live', was married to Ralph Nash in this church in 1936. In her book, Grace writes about how she and her family were captured by the Japanese and interned at both Santo Tomas and Los Baños prison camps.

The compound was an area of two blocks and was not walled in. It included this church building which was used primarily for Sunday services and prayer meetings. There were several residential houses, where missionaries and their families lived. At least one building was like a dormitory with classrooms inside.

"The missionaries provided schooling. My dad taught math and I know we had English and all that kind of thing. Who better to teach than a bunch of missionaries?'

"The religious section of the Japanese Army monitored the Sunday services for content, making sure religious themes were adhered to. We kids all had to attend Sunday church and wear shoes. Well one time I went barefoot which was normal everyday practice and my dad caught me. However, I don't remember any punishment.'

Rumors on how the war was going were rampant and the local news from Japanese sources was always biased. But they received some valid news from San Francisco by an illegal shortwave radio. The news they liked to hear sounded like the Americans were just around the corner and it wouldn't be very long before they arrived. This was more hope than reality.

The MacDonalds and other missionary families spent two years under this type of house arrest, with the relative freedom they enjoyed. Then things started to change.

Chapter Six

Bound for Los Baños

Starting in July of 1944, the war was going badly for the Japanese. They decided they could not afford the liability of a bunch of foreign missionaries being out and around with this much freedom. So, on the 8th of July, late in the afternoon the MacDonalds and others from so-called 'enemy alien' nations, would be returned to prison camps immediately.

They were allowed to take a minimum number of bags with them—two suitcases, a mattress and a bed per person. They spent most of that night packing and sorting out, getting ready for pickup in the morning.

Next morning they were loaded onto trucks and transported back to the Santo Tomas Internment Camp. They slept in the gymnasium that evening.

At five the next morning they were taken to the train station for travel to the Los Baños Internment Camp. Los Baños was located about 35 miles southeast of Manila, at the southern end of a large lake called Laguna de Bay.

The camp was started about ten months earlier when 800 American men from the Santo Tomas Internment Camp were sent down there to begin construction. The camp was built on the former campus grounds of the University of the Philippines Agricultural College. [4]

Upon arrival the MacDonalds were billeted in the southern portion of the camp. George's family along with other missionaries and their families were placed in barracks #17. They were somewhat segregated from the rest of the Americans, but were never informed why this was done. "With Priests, Nuns, Brothers, Protestant Pastors, wives and children, we soon became known to the other part of the camp as the 'Holy City' or the 'Vatican.'" [5]

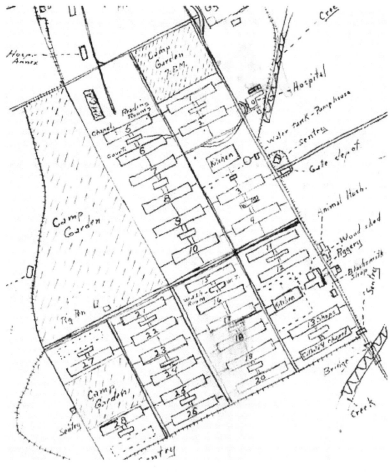

Barracks 17 can be seen on this map drawn by Leo Stancliff, who lived in the same barracks. He also shows who lived in each cubicle.

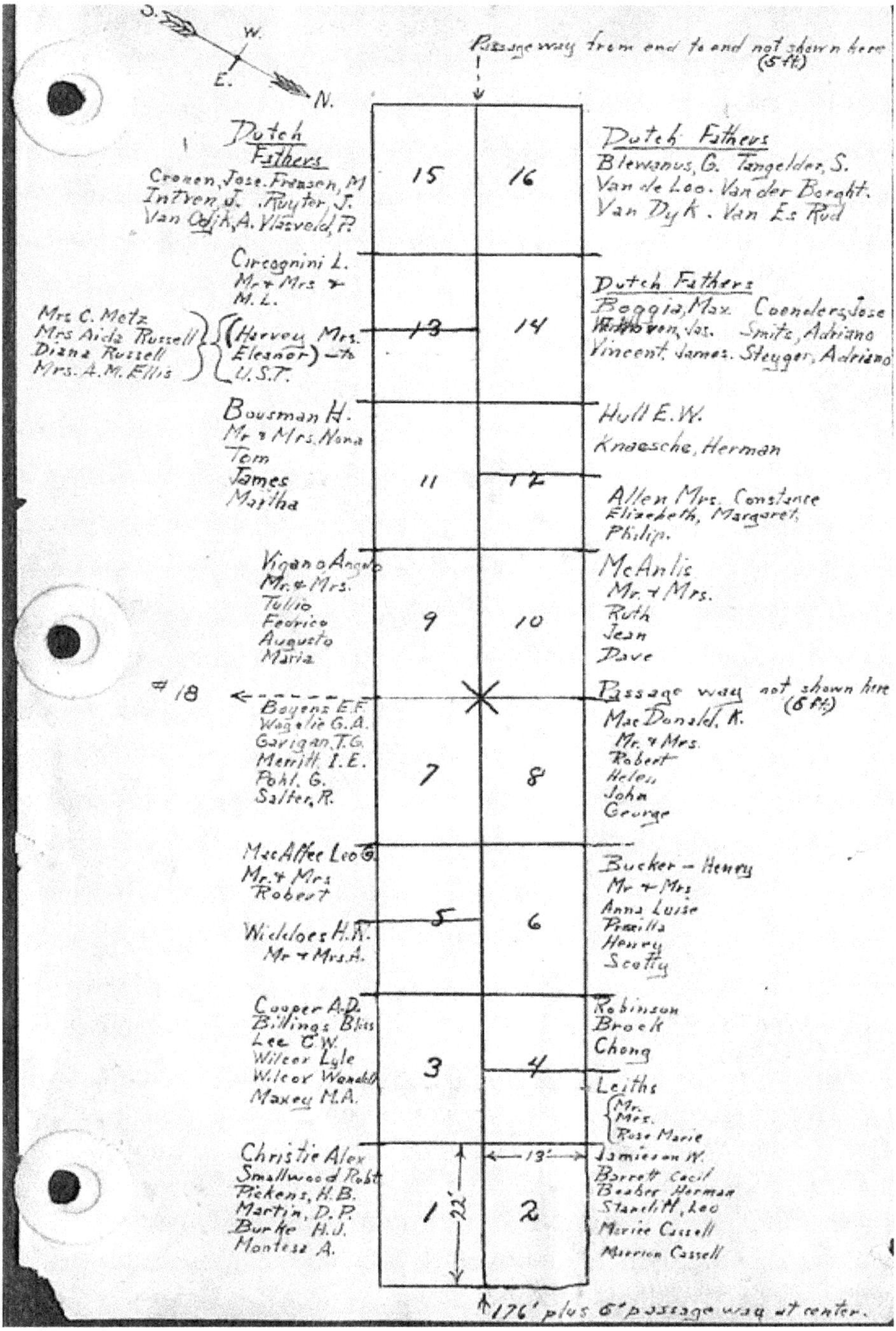

O.
W.
E.
N.

Passage way from end to end not shown here (5 ft)

Dutch Fathers
Cronen, Jose. Freasen, M
Intven, J. Ruyter, J.
Van Odijk, A. Vlasveld, P.

| 15 | 16 |

Dutch Fathers
Blewanus, G. Tangelder, S.
Van de Loo. Van der Borght.
Van Dyk. Van Es. Rud

Circognini L.
Mr & Mrs &
M.L.

Mrs C. Metz
Mrs Aida Russell
Diana Russell
Mrs. A.M. Ellis
} (Hervey, Mrs.
Elesnor) — to
U.S.T.

| 13 | 14 |

Dutch Fathers
Boggia, Max. Coenders, Jose
Withoven, Jos. Smits, Adriano
Vincent, James. Steyger, Adriano

Bousman H.
Mr & Mrs. Nona
Tom
James
Martha

| 11 | 12 |

Hull E.W.
Knaesche, Herman

Allen Mrs. Constance
Elizabeth, Margaret,
Philip.

Vigano Angelo
Mr. & Mrs.
Tullio
Fedrico
Augusto
Maria

| 9 | 10 |

McAntis
Mr. & Mrs.
Ruth
Jean
Dave

#18 ← — — — — — —

Boyens E.F.
Wagelie G.A.
Garigan, T.G.
Merritt I.E.
Pohl. G.
Salter, R.

| 7 | 8 |

✕

Passage way not shown here (6 ft)

MacDonald. K.
Mr. & Mrs.
Robert
Helen.
John
George

MacAffee Leo G.
Mr. & Mrs
Robert

Wicheloes H.A.
Mr. & Mrs. A.

| 5 | 6 |

Bucker — Henry
Mr. & Mrs
Anna Luise
Priscilla
Henry
Scotty

Cooper A.D.
Billings Bliss
Lee C.W.
Wilcor Lyle
Wilcor Wendell
Maxey M.A.

| 3 | 4 |

Robinson
Brock
Chong

Leiths
{ Mr.
Mrs.
Rose Marie

Christie Alex
Smallwood Robt
Pickens, H.B.
Martin, D.P.
Burke H.J.
Montesa A.

| 1 | 2 |

← 13' →
22'

Jamieson W.
Barrett Cecil
Beaber Herman
Standliff, Leo
Marie Cassell
Maurice Cassell

↑ 176' plus 6' passage way at center.

Leo Stancliff lived in cubicle # 2 and the six from the MacDonald family lived in cubicle #8. Shown as Mr. and Mrs. K. MacDonald plus Robert, Helen, John, and George.

Each barracks could hold 80 to 100 internees, and had been built in pairs with a wash room and toilets between them. They were 180 feet in length and contained 16 cubicles, measuring 12'x22' with no walls, just sawali curtains made of leaves woven together, to separate one cubicle from the other.

Here's a typical setup in one of the cubicles. *Drawn by Leo Stancliff.*

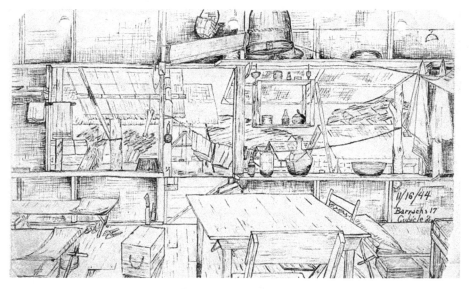

"Dad, later on, got permission to triple bunk the boys' beds, saving valuable floor space."

George remembers it was somewhat unique living in the 'Holy City' in that "We didn't worry about thievery or anything like that and everyone got along well with each other. The Priests and the Sisters pitched in and helped out initiating classes. Father Alfred taught tumbling, which I enjoyed. It was one of those activities to keep kids occupied and out of trouble."

The camp kitchen provided everyone with two meals a day, a minimum amount of food. Initially they started out with 1200 calories a day. They also planted a garden to provide supplemental food and were able in certain cases to buy extra food, but it became extremely expensive. Money was very scarce so we only had a tantalizingly small amount of extra food.

There were over 2,100 internees at Los Baños with 1,600 Americans making up the majority. The next largest contingents were the British, followed by Australians, Canadians, Dutch, Norwegian, Polish and Italian. *See Appendix D for the complete list.*

Chapter Seven

Daily Life at Los Baños

Early on the Japanese allowed and even encouraged the internees to set up a governing structure among themselves. A camp committee was formed to assign work, maintain discipline, settle disputes, dole out food and act as the primary interface between the internees and the Japanese camp commandant. As can be seen from Leo Stancliff's drawing of the camp, the internees initially had 3 large garden spaces to grow fresh vegetables.

While almost all of the internees were civilians there were eleven U.S. Navy nurses among them. They were the only U.S. Active Military in the camp and had been captured in Manila. Upon arrival they set out to convert one of the old barracks into a hospital. Laura Cobb was the Chief Nurse. She and her nurses worked with Dr. Dana Nance who became the medical director for the camp in 1943.

There was also a very large contingent of priests, seminarians, sisters and clergy of all denominations. Included were 98 Catholic Sisters, 53 from the Maryknoll Missionary.

"A couple of months after we got there, in Oct. 1944, each person's daily food intake was down to 880 calories. In addition to the few calories that each person received, the diet was extremely deficient in protein. Certain things that people tried eating were things you'd never imagine. Among them were garden slugs that my Dad found on our plants. They were prepared by soaking them in brine and then frying them. The taste was slightly nutty, as if it was a nut and not the mental state of the person eating it.'

A hint at what prison life was like at Los Baños during this treacherous time can better be illustrated by the words of other prisoners in the camp, starting with the nurse LTJG Dorothy Still.

LTJG Dorothy Still: *LTJG Still was among the eleven Navy nurses captured by the Japanese in Manila and imprisoned at Santo Tomas and then Los Baños.*

Dorothy remembers what life was like and how it changed from the very beginning of the internment camp until the freeing of the prisoners. [6]

"In May 1943, the Japanese sent 800 men from Santo Tomas to Los Baños to set up the camp. Two doctors who were going asked our chief nurse if we would go down and help them set up a little hospital. We weren't needed at Santo Tomas anymore due to the influx of Army nurses after the fall of Corregidor.'

"We initially had two American civilian doctors, but they were repatriated in August 1943. In their place we got another American doctor, Dr. Dana Nance. He was a young fellow, one of those charismatic characters who got out there with the baseball teams and was very concerned about his patients. He was a surgeon and brought his own instruments. Patients who had been sent back to Manila for surgery were now handled in our hospital. We also had a dentist.'

"Initially, there were only the men and nurses at Los Baños. The dependents were supposed to come in July, but did not arrive until December. When they did, they changed the whole outlook of the camp. They brought touches of civilization with them - tablecloths and salt and pepper shakers, etc. Life itself was not that bad. People had the opportunity to exercise, to go out and cut wood, and do chores that needed to be done to keep the community going. People had recordings they played at the bandstand. And they had baseball games. It was really country club living compared to the other camps.'

"While food was not plentiful, at least at this time, starvation was not a problem. Since we lived in an old agricultural college, we had some limited access to meat. We had carabao [water buffalo] mainly, and some pigs. We also had a garden in which we grew mostly eggplants and camotes, a sort of sweet potato. Of course, there was rice as usual and mongo beans. Duck eggs were occasionally available.'

"Life began to change in late 1943. when the Japanese military took over the camps. Before, the camps had been run by Japanese civilian administrators. But now there was a supply officer, LT [Sadaaki] Konishi, who had made life miserable for the internees in Santo Tomas. He apparently wanted to starve the internees there. He came to Los Baños in 1944 to make life miserable for us too. Moreover, our lifestyle worsened appreciably in early 1944 because the Japanese brought many more civilians into Los Baños. Many of the new civilians - the sick and the elderly - had previously been allowed to stay in their homes in Manila.'

And then the whole spirit at Los Baños changed. "There was no more country club living. By this time, the Americans had invaded the Philippines, so as life got worse for the Japanese, they made life worse for us. We were only getting two meals a day, skimpy meals at that. We mainly had rice, diluted to a pasty lugao. There was practically no meat in the stew; it was very watery. And, of course, we used to have coconut milk, but the coconuts had gotten so expensive they were no longer available. We began to lose weight.'

"It looked like Christmas 1944 would be very gloomy, but a songfest by the priests and sisters livened things up. On Christmas Eve they had a midnight mass and practically the whole camp turned out. It was the most spectacular mass I've ever seen. There were no gifts involved on Christmas Day, just a spirit of friendliness between people. It had more meaning than ever before. It was a beautiful Christmas!'

LTJG Dorothy Still was the nurse who assisted Dr. Nance in delivering the youngest baby in the camp, Lois McCoy, on 20 February 1945 during a touch-and-go delivery resulting in the mother suffering severe birth complications.

Sister Miriam Louise Kroeger: *Sister Kroeger was one of the Maryknoll nuns. She describes her life in Los Baños, while living in 'Vatican City.'* [7]

"A fence was erected between us and the other 1,800 prisoners who had preceded us to Los Baños. Our group included 2 bishops, 1 monsignor, 140 priests, and more than a hundred Sisters. The Protestants numbered about 200 missioners.'

"The water system was so regulated that about the only time you would be able to get any water was at midnight or later. Half-sick, starved, nerve-racked prisoners dragged themselves out of bed to wash their clothes and at the same time to use their one and only container to get a little water with which to wash the 'dishes' the next day.'

"Medicines which had been sent by the Red Cross were confiscated by the Japanese, and we were left easy victims to the various epidemics which had such a devastating effect upon the people, mentally as well as physically—malaria, dysentery, infantile paralysis, skin diseases, etc.'

"During the last few months, our food consisted of two cups of lugao, a paste made of four-fifths water and one-fifth rice. This was filled with worms, sand, and stone. In the beginning we cleaned the rice before it was cooked, but later we were so weak that we hadn't the energy to do even that. Some people removed the worms from the cooked rice, but when they finished eating, they were still so starved that they ate the worms which they had previously put aside.'

"No lights were permitted in the camp. This restriction alone was a source of torture, and night traffic in the camp finally became such that our committee had to establish traffic rules whereby everyone kept to his right to avoid the others whom he could not see coming from the opposite direction. Not being able to read at night was another keen punishment; magazines and newspapers were never seen.'

"With the ever-increasing bombing of the islands by the Americans, the camp enclosure became more rigid and the Japanese more difficult to deal with. The final touch came when we were confined to our barracks twenty-four hours a day. When the planes were overhead, we were forbidden to show any emotion; disobeying such a directive meant death by gunfire. As we well knew, there would be no hesitation about shooting. Our men had been warned that anyone found leaving the camp would be shot on sight.'

"The next day at dawn a starving man was found trying to get food over the fence and was killed instantly. Later, another man was returning with a pack of food on his back; he was shot but did not die. When the priest asked permission to see him, the Japanese refused. We saw this man being carried out beyond the gate and heard a shot fired later.'

"Beriberi was of such long standing that it was beginning to endanger everyone's life. Death also resulted from eating weeds that were not considered digestible. Intestinal obstruction resulted. One man who was mentally disturbed tried to eat his mattress and mosquito net. He died. In fact, all of the more than 2,100 could watch the progressing symptoms of the disease in themselves and wonder how much longer they could endure.'

"Despite conditions, we did our best to celebrate Christmas of '44. One of the Canadian brothers made Nativity figures out of clay, with a dirty pink blanket as a backdrop. From our tin cans that were no longer usable, we cut bells and animals to hang on the 'Christmas tree.' It was at times such as this that the Japanese would become very irritated. For all the force and power that lay behind them, they were never able to dampen our spirits. More than once they told us that we were not to be happy because we were prisoners of war and as such had nothing to be merry about. That was one order we never obeyed.'

"Finally the weed patch was closed to us. Bishop then directed that we have exposition of the Blessed Sacrament with public recitation of the rosary throughout the day. Personally I was just so weak that I couldn't even move my fingers from one bead to the other, so I just wrapped the rosary around my wrist and sat out the time."

During the internment Sister Kroeger lost forty pounds but after the rescue, she returned immediately to Baguio in the Philippines and her love for teaching. Later she was asked, along with others, to submit to the War Claims Court her request for refunds. She asked for sixty pesos, forty of which were to replace her office books. She made this low claim in conscience, to the consternation of her Superiors. She thought the clothing she had carried in her small bag

41

was still usable. This is the same Louise who sewed her own clothing. Thursday morning March 9, 1989 at 1:30 A.M. Sister Mary Louise died at Phelps Memorial Hospital in North Tarrytown, New York. [8]

Grace C. Nash: *Grace wrote the book, "That We Might Live", where she tells the story of how her husband and three children overcame the odds and were able to survive both Santo Tomas as well as the Los Baños prison camps. She and Ralph had three sons, Stan, Gale and Roy. Roy their youngest was born while they were in captivity.* [9]

June, 1944: "For some time I had wanted to give a serious musical program in Los Baños. Now with encouragement from a number of internees, I persuaded Rosemary Parquette, a splendid pianist to accompany me. There was a reasonable sounding piano in the empty barracks down by the guard house where we could practice.'

"Outside, the fierce heat beat down on the nipa-thatched roofs of our barracks that stretched in rows along the foothills of the Makiling Mountains. Together we made our way to the empty barracks at the far end of the camp, Rosemary carrying my violin and music, I carrying Roy. Ralph was doing camp work.'

"Inside, we carefully closed the heavy barn-like door. While Rosemary dusted off the rickety piano, I cleared a section of the slag floor where Roy could play, then took out my violin and tuned to a questionable "A" from the piano.'

< *Grace with son Roy*

"We began the concerto. During Rosemary's piano interlude I glanced down at Roy. He was listlessly putting pieces of slag into his tin cup. His sweet face . . . his spindly legs . . . The despair I felt, found expression in the slow throbbing tones of the Adagio Movement of the Bruch Concerto I was playing.'

"But my thoughts were on the coconut trees and banana palms beyond the high fence — heavy with fruit. I thought of Stan and Gale out searching for weeds and scraps of Japanese garbage, of Ralph working an additional two hours in burning sun for an extra cup of rice. Lt. Konishi knew how to break one's spirit and morale, how to procure civilian labor with enforced starvation! All at once a shadow crossed my vision at the entranceway. My bow scratched and bounced off the string. A Japanese soldier was staring at me from inside the barracks door! Still playing, I drew Roy back to me. Rosemary's hands faltered over the keys . . . but we must not stop.'

"The soldier's boots crunched against the slag as he came slowly toward us. A sickening wave of fear swept over me as I struggled on with meaningless notes. It was too late to get Roy and run. We were trapped, and no one would hear our screams. His heavy breathing was close, he was standing over me sucking in his pleasure. I jumped with fright as he shouted. 'Play Mozart!'

"Minuet from Don Juan," I whispered, "Key of C. The guard backed away, grinning and sucking noisily. As we reached the last note, he cried, 'Beethoven!'

"We began the 'Minuet in G.' Rocking slowly with the music, his eyes never shifted. I could feel them staring at me. We played on, praying that he ask no more.'

"The piece was finished. I would put my violin away, gather up Roy and get out. But he rushed toward us, uttering sharp, incoherent phrases. A few feet from me, he stopped and clapping his hands, the Japanese words spilled out, *'Dom arigato, dom arigato!'*

"Bowing low, he backed his way out of the barracks, his bayonet scraping against the slag as he disappeared. We stared after him.'

"He had said, 'Thank you.'

Willie Jamieson: *He was one of four missionaries living in cubicle 2, barracks 17.*

"The food got worse and worse. They took one third of our rice and gave it to their soldiers. The Japanese soldiers would steal the remaining rice in the storehouse, bring it to us and trade it to us for our personal possessions. At that time, Leo traded a 20 Jewel Elgin watch for twelve pounds of soy beans. We ground them to make them go farther. On another occasion, Leo, seeing a dog dragging the bone of a Water Buffalo across the yard, ran after the dog, retrieved the bone, and from it we made a soup sufficient to last several days. Our Committee figured we had food enough to last until February 15, but decided to lessen the ration to make it last until the 19th, hoping the American Army would break through and release us.'

"Knowing the American Army was near, some of the internees escaped to the American lines and told them we had only food enough to last until the 19th. They also told them of the conditions existing in the camp, eighty percent suffering from beriberi, and many dying daily.'

Willie Jamieson concludes. "Almost, every night, as the American forces drew nearer Manila, a number of the Internees would gather outside their cubicles and watch the flashes of gunfire in the distance. Everyone knew his pulse beat for a minute. As the flash of gunfire was observed, each man would grab his wrist, count the pulse beat until the sound of the explosion reached his ear. Knowing the speed of sound, we could, with a little figuring, determine the distance to the guns and the Army's daily advance." [10]

John MacDonald: *George's older brother John recounts his capture and life at Los Baños.*

John was 13 1/2 when his family fled to the hills. "We were going to hide for two or three weeks until the Americans kicked the Japanese out of the country. "That strategy worked until the morning of July 15, 1942. John was in bed, recuperating from an illness. His younger brother George was at a spring, bathing. His mother was setting out tomato plants.

"That morning, I knew I was dead. I didn't know if it would be by machine gun or by a Japanese sword taking off my head. But I knew I was dead."

From that moment forward, MacDonald shut down his emotions. He said "We never stopped believing we would be liberated, but did stop imagining when that day would come. It was always some day, some day. My dad's motto was, "Keep on keepin' on."

"The last few weeks before the Los Baños raid, people in the camp began to die of starvation." He noted that in his father's journal, the Rev. MacDonald wrote of one man's death on Feb. 20th 1945, 'The first thing we heard this morning was that Rev. Herbert E. Blair died about 6 a.m., apparently in his sleep. He was paralyzed from the waist down … His death was due to starvation.' The rations got less and less. I weighed 95 pounds when we were rescued." [11]

45

John MacDonald as well as his father kept diaries in their months at Los Baños. His father wrote of pounding the husks off rice called palay, the only food provided by the sadistic Sadaaki Konishi in the waning days prior to their rescue. His father wrote, "We all were completely done up when night came. When I flopped my head on the pillow about 8:30 the hole in the roof let the light of a brilliant star hit me exactly in the right eye. It was such a wonderful coincidence, I immediately said to myself, 'Another star of Bethlehem,' that is a good omen and can only mean our speedy deliverance. Alas, son John came over and investigated and showed me that it was the light from the moon which was overhead. However I went to sleep feeling that deliverance was near and thanking God for the prospect."

John MacDonald is a soft-spoken man who went on to fly 130 combat missions over Communist lines in Korea, followed by 10 years in B-47 jet bombers during the Cold War before completing a 20-year Air Force career while stationed in Japan supporting U.S. troops in Vietnam. He retired to his mother's hometown of Missoula, MT and is in his 42nd year in the ministry program Spiritual Discovery at prisons in Deer Lodge, Shelby and Walla Walla, Washington.[11]

Lois Bourinskie: *Lois Kathleen McCoy, was the youngest POW of the Los Baños Internment Camp having been born three days before the camp was liberated.* [12]

"Well, both my father and mother were first in Santo Tomas prison camp in Manila and then in the Los Baños prison camp. They were both Americans working in the Philippines before the war."

< Lois in her early 20s.

"I was also a POW, having been born in Los Baños three days before the camp was liberated on Feb. 23rd, 1945. I am the youngest POW rescued from this camp."

"Like most POW's my parents did not like to talk about it. They were engaged to be married in 1940, but were not allowed to marry until April 18th, 1944. It is amazing how anybody could live under those conditions and survive, let alone get married and have a child."

Lois' parents, Oscar Gervius "Mac" McCoy and Mildred Ailene Palmer were married on Apr. 18, 1944 in the Los Baños Internment Camp. Oscar was 35 and Mildred was 27 at the time of their marriage. [34]

Years after the rescue her parents would tell her stories about the ruthless Warrant Officer Sadaaki Konishi. But they also said that some guards were kind, sneaking food to some children to take back to their parents in a detailed secret way.

"My mother was in the infirmary of the camp, having just had me, the newborn baby girl. Dr. Nance, actually delivered me. My mother had complications, so it was a Navy nurse who helped deliver me and cared for me until the rescue."

"My Dad weighed 88 pounds at the rescue and Mom suffered from many diseases. She would have died a horrible death of a burst bladder, had not the rescue happened when it did."

"Thank heaven, General MacArthur made the decision to prioritize rescue operations. The Japanese soldiers became more and more sadistic and were starving the POW's. We were due to be burned alive on the very day of the rescue. I lived in the Philippines with my parents and sisters until I was nearly seven. My parents had a total of seven children! I was the oldest of 4 other sisters and 2 brothers. Both my parents lived past their 90th birthday." [12]

U.S. Airplanes bring hope.

Anytime airplanes would come over the kids would always run to the nearest acacia tree and climb up as high as they could, to get the best view. This was definitely against camp regulations, but they did it anyway. George MacDonald said, "We kept getting chastised for doing it but we enjoyed seeing the airplanes, knowing it was an indication that Americans were getting closer every day.'

Christmas day 1944: "Coming out of chapel after service, we saw these American planes go overhead and by the configuration of the twin booms, we knew they were P-38s.[13] It just thrilled us. Strangely enough, ten years later as I was serving in the Air Force, I happened to be flying across the Pacific, ferrying an airplane back to the States, with an older pilot. One evening between flights we were sitting on Kwajalein Island, just talking, and it came around to my experiences during the war, and he said that he had flown P-38s in the Pacific and the Philippines during that time period. I said, 'You know this one instance on Christmas day that I remember, it was about 11 o'clock and we were coming out of chapel and I saw these P-38s going over,' and he said, 'I was flying one of those.' Strange coincidence."

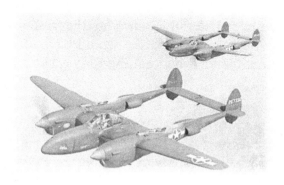

P-38 Lightning fighter aircraft

By that same Christmas of 1944, MacArthur had landed his forces in the central part of the Philippines on the island of Leyte, and had advanced up the island chain to Mindoro. They were using it as a forward air strip for air cover for the forthcoming landings on the island of Luzon.

On the first of January, George recalled seeing some Japanese airplanes going south, and when they later returned to the north, they had holes in their control surfaces. "It turned out that they were the last Japanese aircraft that we saw."

"On Saturday night the 6th of January in the evening, rumors started to fly that it looked like our guards were packing up to leave. It was true and it left us without any guards whatsoever. Immediately the camp committee told all internees to stay put, as they didn't want over 2000 prisoners wandering around the jungle with the Japanese still in the area. If prisoners started running around doing things on their own, a bunch would be killed.'

"The next day was a grand and glorious morning. Someone had an American flag and someone else had a British flag and recordings were played of our National Anthem and 'God Save The King'. A rousing ceremony was held out in front of the barracks where the flags were raised and we all sang the national anthems.'

"After the Japanese left, the camp committee put out feelers and made contact with Filipinos in the local area to obtain food; signing notes to pay for it. This put the lie to the Japanese statements that there wasn't any food in the area. We got more than a sufficiency of food during the absence of the Japanese.'

"But the following Saturday they came back. Not the original guards but second line troops. They were older, or had been wounded and not completely fit for front line duty, or they had been used to build fortifications for the defense of Manila.'

"We never knew why they left but when the guards heard about all that had happened in the camp while they were gone, they really searched for those flags. Fortunately, the flags were well hidden and not found. In fact, that American flag is still in existence, belonging to the daughter of one of the prisoners, who now lives in Oklahoma.'

"During our freedom week someone had a hidden radio, brought it out, connected it up and for the first time in years we got news straight from the USA. It was definitely heartening to us. This week of freedom saved many people including my dad but despite this fact, from that time until our rescue, many people died of starvation. Two of our missionaries died within three days of our rescue.'

Warrant Officer Sadaaki Konishi was largely responsible for the starvation of the internees. He was in charge of food and supplies and purposely began the month to month reduction of food, resulting in the increasing deaths of internees due to starvation. He was hated by all of the internees because of his sadistic and brutal nature.

The camp commandant was a weak willed individual. So he let Konishi enforce discipline and carry out punishments.

On the night of 27 January 1945 George Louis made his way out of camp to find food. On his return the next morning a guard spotted him and shot him in the shoulder. A catholic priest and the internees' camp doctor asked permission to help him but were denied. Sometime later as Louis lay on the ground, the camp commandment and Konishi walked over to him. Konishi took his gun out of its holster, gave it to one of the soldiers. That soldier went over to Louis and shot him in the head. [14]

Chapter Eight

Vanderpool and the Guerrillas

Major Jay Vanderpool and Filipino guerrillas had a unique role in rescuing the POWs in Los Baños.

Vanderpool covertly entered Luzon by submarine two months before MacArthur's forces landed on the beaches of Lingayen Gulf. His broad sweeping order from MacArthur was, "Do what will best further the Allied cause."

His main goal was to coordinate with the Filipino guerrillas, to bring together their various disparate units into a more effective fighting force, to have them collect intelligence that he could forward to MacArthur's headquarters, and ensure that they were well equipped with weapons, ammo, and other supplies.

Jay was born in Wetumka, Oklahoma, in 1917. His father's ancestry claims Dutch and Flemish heritage, while his mother's side claims mixed American Indian heritage. Short and stocky but strong from his days as a high school football player and as an amateur boxer in the U.S Army, he was very comfortable with the outdoor

51

life and would often go out on his own, for days at a time, with a backpack, rifle, and fishing pole. He well knew his way around the backcountry and mountains of Oklahoma. [15]

Jay enlisted in the Army in 1936 at the age of 19. He attained the rank of Staff Sergeant in the Field Artillery, then went to Officer Candidate School (OCS) and received a 2nd lieutenant commission on 5 April 1941. He was then assigned to the 8th Field Artillery Battalion, at Schofield Barracks, Hawaii. He survived the Japanese attack on Pearl Harbor and Wheeler Airfield, and then went on to fight at Guadalcanal with the 11th Marine Regiment and the 25th Infantry Division. [16]

During his time in Guadalcanal, Vanderpool was a participant in a joint Army and Navy program for selected officers to teach them how to survive in the wilderness. They were taught scouting techniques, map reading, navigating by compass, first aid, and how to best construct a temporary encampment under little or no shelter. Each officer had to lead a platoon sized unit from coast to coast across the mountain ranges of Guadalcanal. At the end of this course of instruction, Captain Vanderpool was selected as the most outstanding patrol leader. [15]

He was promoted to Major and his division made him the Assistant G-2 (Intelligence officer.) In this capacity he taught soldiers scouting and patrolling and in general, how to survive in the jungle.

Bruce Henderson describes Vanderpool's teachings in his book "Rescue at Los Baños: The Most Daring Prison Camp Raid of World War II" where he states,

"He taught his men how to keep from getting sick in the jungle, how to care for their feet in the wet environment, how to make a fire in a rain forest, how to set up a lean-to and dry out their clothes at night, and tricks such as not stopping to rest after crossing a river—which would stiffen cold muscles—but to go to the next ridge before taking a break. But it was more than being trained for the jungle—it was also about developing the confidence to face an enemy experienced in jungle fighting." [15]

Whether he became tired of teaching or just wanted to move on to something more challenging, Vanderpool volunteered to become one of many 'agents' to be inserted into the Philippines to gain intelligence on Japanese force positions and movements.

With MacArthur's vague guidance to "do what you think will best further the Allied cause," Vanderpool went aboard the attack submarine USS Cero, headed for Luzon. On the night of 2 November 1944 Vanderpool deboarded the Cero at the mouth of the Masanga River in East Luzon. He then rowed to a remote jungle beach. There, he linked up with his contact, Lt. Colonel Bernard Anderson, leader of a large sized local guerrilla unit. Anderson was one of many Americans able to escape and evade capture by the Japanese and form resistance groups.

The USS Cero (SS-225) delivered fourteen soldiers and twenty tons of cargo in three separate covert landings on Luzon in the Philippines between 25 October and 2 November 1944. (U.S. Navy photo)

Vanderpool then went on a hazardous jungle journey, hiding in churches and homes until he reached Laguna de Bay. He avoided Japanese patrol boats on the Bay and finally reached the ROTC Hunters, a Filipino-led guerrilla force in the region south of Manila. While there he worked to bring feuding guerrilla groups in the area into a cohesive alliance against the Japanese.

53

Michael E. Krivdo, PhD who wrote the paper, "Major Jay D. Vanderpool - Advisor to the Philippine Guerrillas" states that,

"Vanderpool lived with the Filipino irregulars for five months, regularly moving among several disparate units to coordinate actions and avoid being captured by the Japanese. His influence expanded as he gradually took full charge. In late 1944 he formed his own General Guerrilla Command (GGC). The increased role of the GGC led Japanese intelligence officers to conclude that Vanderpool was a major general in command of multiple guerrilla units and they expended great time and energy to find him. Furthermore, Vanderpool's fighters provided quality information, making them invaluable to MacArthur's command after the U.S. landings on Luzon in January 1945." [17]

Luzon Philippine guerrillas turn over two Japanese prisoners of war (POWs) to soldiers of the 25th Infantry Division.

His most important words to the many Guerrilla units he worked with were, "Don't go jumping into taking on the Japanese Army by yourselves, because if you are wiped out you are no good to anyone."

During the Japanese occupation there were numerous resistance groups all over the Philippines. The following were located locally in Luzon and had major roles in freeing the Los Baños POWS.

Hunter's ROTC Guerrillas.

Vanderpool's primary interface was with the Hunter's ROTC Guerrillas. Many Hunter's had been sergeants or officers in the Philippine Scouts and the rest were cadets in the former Filipino Military Academy. The Hunters commander was Eleuterio L. 'Terry' Adevoso, a former Philippine Army Cadet. The Hunters were considered the most powerful guerrilla group.

PQOG (President Quezon's Own Guerillas)

Vanderpool also assumed responsibility for several other guerrilla units in the area.[66] Including the PQOG (President Quezon's Own Guerillas) which was commanded by Romeo Espino. Espino's nom-de-guerre was 'Colonel Price.'

Hukbalahap Guerrillas

The Hukbalahaps were a resistance group that had a political agenda. Often shortened to "Huks," they consisted of Filipinos from all backgrounds - peasant farmers, workers' union members, communist party members and rural and urban laborers. They killed many Japanese soldiers and the Huks also targeted rich Filipinos who collaborated with the Japanese. Their leader was Luis Taruc.

Marking Fil-American Guerrillas

This group was led by Colonel Marcos V. Agustin (aka Marcos Marking.) Compared to the younger ROTC guerrillas, the guerrilla fighters who were recruited under Colonel Agustin, tended to be older civilians and soldiers who were both tenacious fighters and strategists. He's shown here with his wife Yay Panlilio, a Filipina-Irish-American who had fought alongside him and his guerrillas. *Photo credit Carl Mydans.*

Chapter Nine

Concern for the POWs

General MacArthur's motivation to save prisoners was one of the most important things that led to their rescue. The Japanese had a policy that was documented and signed by General Yamashita indicating to commanders throughout his theater that if they still had prisoners and the American soldiers were coming close, there would be nothing to prevent them from just executing those prisoners.

Prior to MacArthur's return to the Philippines he became aware of three prison camps. The military camp up north at Cabanatuan, in Manila at Bilibid, as well as civilians at Santo Tomas. When he learned of the existence of the Los Baños camp from guerrilla intelligence sources, MacArthur also found out the grizzly details of an incident involving U.S. POWs on Palawan.

The Palawan Massacre

Known as the Palawan Massacre, it confirmed intercepted Japanese cables containing orders to kill all surviving POWs before American troops advanced. The orders stated:

"(a) Whether they are destroyed individually or in groups or however it is done, with mass bombing, poisonous smoke, poisons, drowning, decapitation, or what, dispose of them as the situation dictates.'

"(b) In any case it is the aim not to allow the escape of a single one, to annihilate them all, and not to leave any traces." [18]

Palawan

In August of 1942, 300 American prisoners of war were brought to Puerto Princesa on Palawan Island to build an airfield. Most of them had survived the infamous Bataan Death March. Interned in Palawan's Prison Camp 10A, they spent two years clearing the land and then built an 8-inch-thick concrete runway. Sick or weak prisoners, no longer able to work, were replaced with healthier POWs from Manila to complete the project. Upon completion in September 1944, half of the prisoners were sent back to Manila. [37,39]

The remaining 150 POWs endured arduous manual labor repairing craters caused by U.S. bombings of the airstrip, while being starved, denied medical care, and routinely and viciously beaten. This cruel behavior increased toward the end of 1944 as it became clear that the Japanese were losing the war. The guards became increasingly short-tempered and carried out cruel punishments for the slightest of infractions. [35,37]

To protect their workforce from U.S. bombings, the Japanese made the prisoners construct shelters. They built three dirt trenches, each 150 feet long and 4 feet high, covered with timbers and two feet of dirt. The openings of the shelters were only large enough to allow entrance of one man at a time. They also built several shelter holes to hold two or three men. [19]

In December, the Americans had a landing force going to invade Mindoro and along their route, they came close to Palawan. When the Japanese sighted those ships, they mistakenly thought they were going to land and make an attempt to liberate the American prisoners.

On December 14th 1944, as the prisoners were repairing damage to the airstrip, they sensed something was wrong. There were many more guards than normal watching them. Around 11:00 AM the POWs were herded into trucks and brought back to Camp10-A. After arriving they heard an air raid alarm and armed guards with fixed bayonets started pushing the prisoners into the trenches. The guards appeared very stressed and mean spirited and would not allow any of the prisoners to look out. Surely something was up. And then it happened. Guards carrying buckets, poured gasoline into the entrance of shelter A, while other guards threw lighted torches into the opening. The prisoners were trapped in a blazing fire. Seven men with skin and clothing ablaze were able to crawl out but were immediately machine-gunned to death. Horrified prisoners who were able to look out from the other shelters told the others packed inside what was happening. [35]

Seeing the guards on their way to shelter B, the men in shelter C knew there was no time to waste and they began digging with their bare hands through the dirt at the end of their trench. When shelter

C was built, the prisoners, with escape in mind had loosened the dirt there as well as outside the trench to the fence line. Beyond that fence there was a 50 to 60 foot drop to a rocky beachline below. A number of prisoners manage to escape trench C just as it was being set ablaze. Altogether about two dozen POWs managed to escape either from the trench or other areas of the camp by sliding down that steep rock cliff. The Japanese took pursuit and managed to hunt down and kill most of the escapees.[35]

The killing continued until nightfall. Those surviving, came out from hiding and several were successful in swimming across the bay to a penal colony where they were fed and clothed by members of the resistance movement.[19] Others, some wounded and injured, made it along the coast and all eleven were subsequently led to safety by Philippine guerillas. Once back in friendly territory these survivors told their horrific stories.[35] This is what prompted MacArthur to make sure prisoners at other POW camps in the Philippines would not undergo the same fate.

A Marine, Glenn McDole, was one of the eleven survivors. Later in life he told his story to Bob Wilbanks, who wrote the book, "Last Man Out - Glenn McDole, USMC, Survivor of the Palawan Massacre in World War II" Here's a photo of the younger McDole.[39]

One of the Japanese guards had kept a diary of the events surrounding the massacre. A day after the massacre he wrote, "They truly died a pitiful death. The ones who worked in the repair shop really worked hard. From today on I will not hear the familiar greeting, 'Good morning, Sergeant Major.' I can no longer greet them in this world." Then on January 9th 1945 he revisited the motor vehicle repair shop and writes, "Today, the shop is a lonely place. The prisoners who were assisting us there are now just white bones on the beach washed by the waves. Furthermore, there are numerous corpses in the nearby garage and the smell is unbearable. It gives me the creeps." [39]

Medical personnel excavating bodies of American soldiers from Shelter A. [35]

One of the uncovered trenches showing the remains.

Puerto Princesa now has a plaque at the site and in 1952, the remains of 123 of the Palawan victims were transferred to the Jefferson Barracks National Cemetery near St. Louis, Mo., where they lie in a mass grave, honored today by the few who remember.

Today, Palawan Island has been described as the most beautiful Island in the world, however American prisoners on the island did not get the chance to appreciate that beauty.

Chapter Ten

MacArthur Returns

It had been more than 2½ years since General MacArthur was ordered by President Roosevelt to leave the Philippines and set-up a new headquarters in Australia. However he promised to return.

In October 1944 he made good on his promise when he, along with a huge fleet of naval vessels, arrived in the Philippines and came ashore on the island of Leyte.

General Douglas MacArthur wades ashore during the Leyte landings with Philippine president Sergio Osmeña (left)

By the autumn of 1944, the war situation had grown worse for Japan. Her position became desperate and the war had reached a stage where another major Japanese defeat would portend the collapse of the Japanese Empire. This would destroy their centuries-old tradition of invincibility. The Philippines probably offered the last chance for the Japanese Army to regain its lost prestige and they desperately needed a victory over General MacArthur's forces. Their hopes to achieve this victory relied on the Japanese navy and their battle fleet. They would have to come to the rescue in full strength in an attempt to counter MacArthur's invasion efforts.[20]

And that they did. The Japanese navy with more strength, speed and firepower than the American fleet engaged in battle with everything they had. For a time it looked like they were winning, then for reasons unknown the Japanese disengaged and pulled back.

But other Japanese attack forces flying from land based airfields were not yet ready to throw in the towel. For the first time the Americans witnessed the suicidal Kamikaze attack pilots and the widespread destruction they caused to U. S. fleet units in the Leyte area.

On 29 October a suicide plane crashed into the carrier Intrepid. The next day, the carriers Franklin and Belleau Wood were struck, resulting in severe damage and loss of life. On 1 November, Kamikaze planes destroyed one destroyer and caused serious hits on five others. Four days later, the aircraft carrier Lexington's signal bridge was blasted by a suicide plane. The necessity of dealing with the dangerous threat of these Kamikaze attacks forced the carriers to commit their planes to their own protection at the expense of furnishing support to the Leyte ground forces.[20]

However, General MacArthur's promise to return to the Philippines was fulfilled. After the main breach landings were completed, he walked ashore and speaking to millions of waiting Filipinos, over a portable radio, he said: [20]

"This is the Voice of Freedom, General MacArthur speaking. People of the Philippines: I have returned. By the grace of Almighty God our forces stand again on Philippine soil-soil consecrated in the blood of our two peoples. We have come, dedicated and committed to the task of destroying every vestige of enemy control over your daily lives, and of restoring, upon a foundation of indestructible strength, the liberties of your people.''

Twice life size, statues of MacArthur's return to the Philippines.

Although MacArthur began his invasion of the Philippines in October of 1944, it would take another three months before a U.S. force would land in Luzon to continue with the complete defeat of the Japanese in the Philippines.

MacArthur's 2nd Landing

On January 9th 1945: General MacArthur made a second landing in Luzon.

The following map shows where MacArthur first landed at Leyte Gulf and his second landing at Lingayen Gulf.

Map annotated by author.

In preparation for the landing, on 6 January the U.S. Navy began neutralization strikes against Japanese installations, especially those that threatened the fleet with suicidal air attacks by Kamikaze aircraft that were so effectively employed at Leyte.

In fact they began their attacks only one day after advance units of the naval task force began their journey from Leyte to Luzon. Japanese Kamikaze planes began to dive into those ships. On 4

January, an escort carrier, was damaged so badly that it had to be sunk.[20]

The following afternoon, six ships suffered hits or damaging near misses. On 6 January, off Lingayen Gulf, the fire support groups were again attacked by the largest and most deadly group of suicide planes encountered during the operation. At least sixteen vessels were struck during the course of the day, resulting in extensive casualties both to ships and personnel.[20]

These suicide pilots had become very skilled and had substantially improved their tactics since the battle of Leyte Gulf. The Japanese pilots were now relatively well trained and their deception measures excellent. They made full use of land masses, and counterfeit identification devices to escape radar detection.[20]

Author's supplied picture from the U.S. Naval Institute [23]

The toll the Kamikazes attacks took on the U.S. military was substantial. It killed more than 2,100 sailors. It sank two dozen ships, and damaged another 67. [21]

As a result of the heavy air opposition by the Japanese, the U.S. Third Fleet, fleet intensified its bombardment and fire support strikes against Luzon. Enemy air attacks began to diminish sharply, indicating that the Japanese were running out of airplanes.[20]

Seventh Fleet warships had accomplished their assigned mission by thoroughly pulverizing the Lingayen beach areas with naval gunfire. Land-based planes of the Fifth Air Force, took up the task of direct support of the amphibious landings.[20]

Japanese suicide boats succeeded in sinking or damaging several of the landing crafts but the landings were successful. The four attack groups, one for each division, were in position off their designated beaches along a front of twelve miles.[20]

The Luzon landing operation was announced by MacArthur in a communique, "Our forces have landed in Luzon. In a far-flung amphibious penetration our troops have seized four beachheads in Lingayen Gulf. The decisive battle for the liberation of the Philippines and the control of the Southwest Pacific is at hand.[20]

MacArthur coming ashore in Lingayen Gulf, Luzon.

Chapter Eleven

Starvation

As the American forces drew closer to Los Baños, the food situation became extremely critical. In the week before their rescue the camp kitchen ceased to operate. There was no food available to cook.

George MacDonald said, "What rice was issued out to individuals was unhusked. You had to husk it yourself and that took a great amount of effort, especially for people who were already suffering from starvation. We used pieces of bamboo and heavy steel, sifted it through a fly swatter and saved everything possible. In fact, to have a little more rice, we took in rice from others to husk, for one third of the rice remaining. I really don't think it was worth it because it was a terrible thing to try to do by hand. It was very time consuming and tedious work, and only resulted in 2 1/2 cups of extra rice for our family that week."

George, quoting from fellow prisoner Grace Nash's book, [9]

"Slow starvation cannot be described. To be understood it must be felt. And further torture in this living death came when they denied us salt. The intense heat which had dehydrated our systems now made us suffer even more without any salt.''

"A mild form of insanity had settled over ninety percent of the camp - the frenzied copying of recipes. I knew that such fanaticism happened to explorers, isolated without sufficient food reserves, but I was determined not to give in to it. Children from 10 yrs. old to feeble, aged men who had never cooked in their lives, were now engaged in recipes! Exchanging, copying, talking recipes, filled their waking hours - but not their stomachs!''

"Recipes, recipes, dreams of food, hallucinations of malted milks, sirloin steaks, Irish potatoes, paraded through my mind. I finally succumbed. Grabbing a pencil stub and Stan's [her son's] worn notebook, I wrote in feverish speed, gathering recipes from other internees to copy in my book. My mouth watered as I scribbled down the ingredients, imagining the supreme joy of eating the whole recipe, myself!"

George MacDonald also had, and still has, a recipe book copied into a modified receipt journal.

Hugh Williams a former British Sea Captain took a liking to Grace's two sons and her baby. To keep morale up he would tell the children tales about pirates.

Then when starvation became acute and everyone felt pain in their stomachs and were suffering from aching joints, due to beriberi, Hugh would often put his own small amount of mush on the boy's plates, saying he really did not care that much for mush.

Grace's breast milk started drying up and baby Roy was so weak it couldn't even cry. One morning, Hugh came to the rescue and gave Grace a container of powdered milk he had been saving from a Red Cross shipment that made it through a year earlier. Grace looked at Hugh, who was now skin and bones and insisted that he needed it himself. He forced her to take it and all he wanted in return was for Grace to play "Danny Boy" at her next concert if there was to be one. Hugh didn't make the concert. He died from acute colitis.

The camp doctor said 'he might have made it if he had been on an all milk diet.' [24]

Sister Kroeger recalls,

"The deaths were reaching such a number that the grave-digging crew had to be doubled in order to prevent the bodies from remaining unburied too long. To watch our men at such work was a gruesome ordeal. Their skeleton frames were clad only in patched shorts, and as they dug laboriously in the claylike soil, their bones moving painfully in harmony with each slow-motion swing of the pick, one wondered if in reality they weren't digging their own resting places."

George MacDonald wondered how long the Los Baños prisoners would have to wait to be rescued, if ever.

"In the time between our freedom week and rescue we had several Americans go in and out of our camp, under the fence, through gullies, to make contact with the Filipino guerrillas. As it turned out this was one of the key factors in our very successful rescue.'

Freddy Zervoulakos, the son of a Greek father and Filipina mother, was the first to risk his life to make contact with the guerrillas. He spoke fluent Tagalog. Escaping under the barb wire on the evening of 12 February, he made it to the home of Helen Espino the wife of the guerrilla Romeo Espino (aka Colonel Price.) While there he met Gustavo "Tabo" Ingles, Vanderpool's coordinator for guerrilla forces. Ingles was a Hunters ROTC guerrilla and on Vanderpool's staff. Ingles gave Freddy a copy of instructions he had received from Vanderpool on 10 February. Those instructions required Tabo to assess the enemy strength and positions at the camp as well as the number of internees and their physical condition. But somewhat alarming it gave Tabo Ingles authority to "order an attack, or await reinforcements." [14]

Freddy again left the camp with two others about a week before their rescue, one of which was spirited to the 11th Airborne

Headquarters, where the planning for the rescue of the camp was in progress.

Those three men were the 21 year old Freddy Zervoulakos, joined by 26 year old Benjamin Franklin "Ben" Edwards and 40 year old Prentice Melvin "Pete" Miles. The three escaped on the evening of 18 February and met up with Romeo Espino (aka Colonel Price) at his guerrilla camp. While there they learned that the U.S. Army was planning a raid and rescue mission for the Los Baños internees and were in dire need of detailed intelligence about the camp. Pete Miles was chosen to make his way to the 11th Airborne Headquarters in Manila and would be escorted by guerrillas. Freddy and Ben would remain behind, but be prepared to make the same trip in case Pete didn't make it. [14]

Pete made it and George remembers that Pete "provided them with minute details: where the guard posts were, fields of fire, and one important fact, that between a quarter to seven and seven fifteen every morning the guards not on duty would be out in the clearing next to their barracks doing calisthenics with their weapons stacked inside the barracks. This provided a perfect opportunity and timing for the raid.'

Dire Warning

February 21st, 1945: Staff Sgt. John Fulton, radio operator attached to a guerrilla unit, was directed by Colonel Price, (Guerrilla, Chief of Staff) to transmit the following teletype message to the 11th Airborne Division.[16] Col. Price was also known as Romeo Espino – the Filipino guerrilla and commander of the PQOG (President Quezon's Own Guerrillas)

URGENT
ESPINO TO VANDERPOOL HAVE RECEIVED
RELIABLE INFORMATION THAT JAPS HAVE LOS
BAÑOS SCHEDULED FOR MASSACRE PD
SUGGEST THAT ENEMY POSITIONS IN LOS
BAÑOS PROPER AS EXPLAINED MILLER BE
BOMBED AS SOON AS POSSIBLE PD

(Teletype messages used Morse code that contained only letters, so the PDs in the message stand for 'periods' at the end of sentences.)

Now more than ever, decisive action needed to be taken. Internees had noted, of late, that Filipino laborers had been digging a huge trench about 300 feet long and very deep, just outside the main gate. [15]

Why? They wondered.

Chapter Twelve

Planning the Rescue

Major General Joseph May Swing who commanded the 11th Airborne Division in the Philippines had been given the mission to free the internees at Los Baños on February 3rd 1945. However it was not an immediate priority for him at the time because his troops were engaged in attacking the Japanese in an effort to free Manila.

The plan of attack and the subsequent rescue of the Los Baños internees was straight forward. It consisted of four main parts and depended heavily on prior intelligence and the element of surprise.

Based on Pete Miles' details and other intelligence information, the 11th Airborne Headquarters staff, was able to construct the following map of the Los Baños internment camp, showing the location of the guard posts and other important intelligence information.

The author included the location of the guards' gun rack. [25]

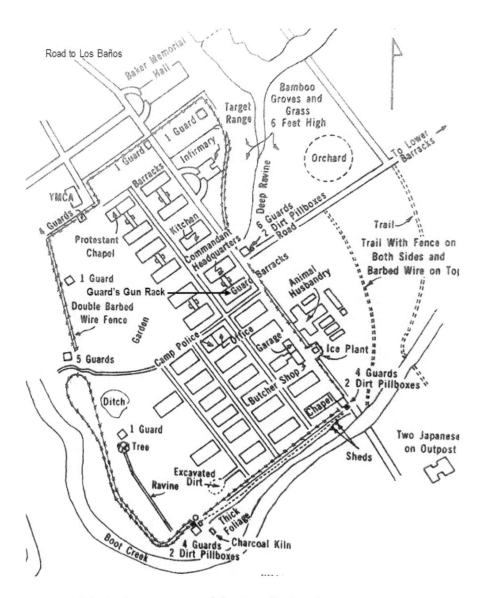

11th Airborne map of the Los Baños internment camp.

On February 18th 1945 Major Henry Burgess, commander of the 1st Paratrooper Battalion, was ordered to withdraw his troops from combat positions and proceed to Manila. Burgess reported to the

11th Airborne Division headquarters, then located at Parañaque, a town in the southern part of Manila.

Burgess met with Colonel Quandt, the Division G-3 (operations officer), who informed him that his battalion would be involved in the rescue of 2,000 civilian prisoners from the Los Baños internment camp. Burgess spent the remainder of the day at headquarters, meeting with division Intelligence and Operations and planning the mission. The next day Burgess met with Pete Miles, who provided information on the layout of the camp and the schedules of the guards. Those were the details necessary to complete the mission precisely and without needlessly endangering the internees.[35]

Burgess' role would be to bring 54 Amtracs [amphibious personnel carriers] across the water to arrive at the internment camp around H-hour, and then take charge of the entire operation to ensure that the internees were safely evacuated.

Lt. General Edward Flanagan in his book "Angels at Dawn - The Los Baños Raid" outlines how Colonel Quandt and his G-3 staff planners had to integrate the following facts and considerations into their tactical plan of operations: [14]

(1) a large number of the internees could not walk for any distance and would have to be transported in some sort of vehicle; in addition, they would have to be evacuated rapidly and promptly;

(2) an all-out, all-guns-blazing assault on the camp would result in needless internee deaths;

(3) the assault, instead, would have to be made with stealth, surprise, daring, and speed;

(4) the withdrawal of the necessarily small and mobile assault forces and the internees could be by water or overland and would have to be made deliberately but with maximum speed before the Japanese in areas close to the camp could react and attack, or set up roadblocks;

(5) the attacking units could assault the camp by land (along National Highway 1 and down the west side of Laguna de Bay), by sea (across Laguna de Bay), and by air (a parachute drop); and

(6) the raiding force would have to be small enough to get in and out promptly but large enough to defeat the opposition, marshal the internees, block any Japanese forces from moving in to reinforce their Los Baños garrison, and move back to their own lines, fighting along the way if necessary.

With those factors and considerations to guide him, Colonel Quandt developed a scheme of attack utilizing all three elements—land, sea, and air. The most salient components of the raiding force and their missions were the following:

1. The division recon platoon [under Lt. Skau] would precede the main body, cross Laguna de Bay in bancas [small sailing vessels with outriggers] shortly before the raid, contact the local guerrillas, coordinate their participation in the raid, position themselves and the guerrillas around the camp, and launch their strike to neutralize the sentries at H-hour [07:00]; the platoon would also, at H-hour, pop smoke grenades to mark the drop zone for the parachuting company and mark the landing site for the amphibious portion of the force. The recon platoon's and accompanying guerrillas' phase of the operation was obviously a key, if not the most crucial, segment in the entire plan of attack.

2. An infantry company (reinforced) would parachute next to the camp, rush immediately to the assistance of the recon platoon and guerrillas in the event they were not able to eliminate all of the guards in the immediate camp area, organize the internees for their evacuation, and set up a perimeter defense of the camp to prevent any Japanese outside the camp attacking it.

3. An infantry battalion, minus the company that would make the parachute assault, but reinforced with an engineer company and two howitzers of an artillery battery, would move across the bay in amphibious tractors. At H-hour the battalion would hit the beach and deploy as rapidly as possible to the camp. Then it would assist the company that had dropped in and deploy one of its companies to the south of the camp to block any element of the Japanese Tiger Division that might move north and another company to the west to block Japanese forces from the Lecheria Hills area. It would set up roadblocks with the help of an engineer platoon that would accompany it and, with their Amtracs, provide an alternate means to evacuate the internees.

4. An overland ground attack by a combat team, composed of an infantry battalion reinforced by two artillery battalions and a company of tank destroyers, would move south from Manila along National Highway 1; attack across the San Juan River near Calamba; block any Japanese forces moving up on the west side of the camp from the Santo Tomas vicinity; move to the camp to reinforce the parachute and amphibious elements in the event the enemy tried to attack in force from the south; and bring with it enough trucks to evacuate the internees overland. These trucks were, in the initial plans, the primary means of hauling out the internees [but Amtracs were used instead.] The staff planned that the overland effort would, in fact, be the main effort in holding off any Japanese counterattacks.

5. Air cover would be available for any assistance required.

6. Guerrilla units would fan out to the west and south of the Los Baños area and block any Japanese forces that might move in to prevent the liberation of the camp or interfere with the evacuation of the internees. [14]

The author constructed the following map showing the most probable planned routes of the attacking forces and the location of a Japanese Infantry Division consisting of 8,000 to 10,000 men. [26]

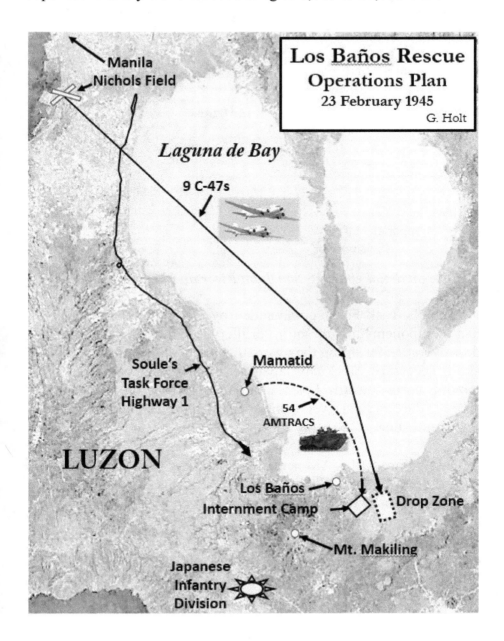

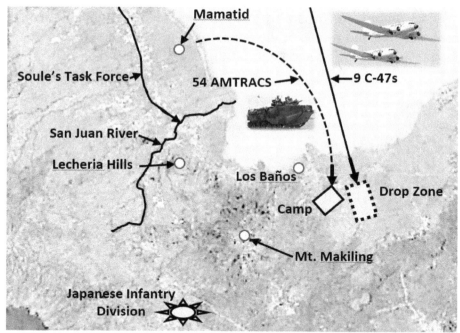

Close up detail showing San Juan River and Lecheria Hills.

Soule's Task Force commanded by Colonel Robert Soule had components of infantry, artillery, engineers, and tank destroyers. 1,500 strong they were to act as a diversionary force and if necessary, block any Japanese from the infantry division moving north towards Los Baños. They arrived on the north shore of the San Juan river on the evening of the 22nd and camped there until sunrise.

Just before 07:00 AM on the 23rd Soule's men spotted the Amtracs and C-47s headed toward the camp and the drop zone. Infantry components then crossed the river engaging the enemy and fighting their way to the stronghold of Lecheria Hills, while other components moved south as a potential blocking force against any Japanese moving north. Another component with Filipino guerrillas moved to neutralize Calamba a Makapili stronghold.

Captain Ken Dawson, the tank-destroyer company commander was killed in this engagement.[15] Lecheria Hills and the surrounding area were taken, but unfortunately, soldiers John T. Doiron and Vernal Ray McMurtrey, were also killed in the fight. [27]

Chapter Thirteen

Airborne Assault and Guerrilla Attack Planning

The key to a successful raid on the Los Baños prison camp was the use of stealth and surprise. Stealth being the use of 11th Airborne reconnaissance members and Filipino guerrillas being in place around the camp, ready to attack at H hour (7:00AM) and surprise being the use of an airdrop of 90 paratroopers in a field next to the camp at the same hour. These two critical tasks were left to two young officers. Lt Ringler and Lt. Skau.

First Lieutenant, John Ringler was given three days' notice to lead his company across Laguna de Bay in nine C-47 airplanes, and then jump, with his paratroopers, into a small field close to the Los Baños internment camp. The field was surrounded on three sides by trees and by high-tension wires on the fourth side.

Ringler was pulled off the front line on 21 February, 1945 for the Los Baños mission. He reported to Major General Swing's office, where he was told that his "B" Company would jump on Los Baños to rescue the internees from the Japanese prison camp. He was told that they could take heavy losses of troops and internees if they were not successful.

Gen Swing discussed the major points of the operation, then he directed his Intelligence Officer (G-2) and Operations Officer (G-3) to provide a complete briefing on the information they had available to them.

As John Ringler remembers, [28]

"It was at this time that I was informed of the other elements that would make up the task force to accomplish the mission. As the air-borne commander, I was permitted to select my own drop zone from the photos that the G-2 and G-3 provided. They also provided a very detailed and complete intelligence summary on the enemy gun positions, diagrams of the camp facilities and a daily routine of activities of the Japanese guards.'

"This information, which was very vital, was provided by Peter Miles, an American internee who escaped from the prison camp a few days earlier. After many hours of briefing and planning, I returned to my unit, which had already been relieved from the front line action.'

"After discussions with the Ist Battalion Commanding Officer, Major Henry Burgess, he attached the Light Machine Gun platoon, under the command of Lt. Walter Hettlinger, to [my] "B" Company to provide extra manpower and fire power.'

"I was briefed that the Ist Battalion (minus "B" Company), with attached units, would travel by Amtracs across the lake (Laguna de Bay).

The 88th Glider Infantry Regiment (minus its 2nd Bn) would establish the diversionary force to hold the enemy in their positions'.

"The Filipino guerrilla force would outpost the outer edge of the prison camp to prevent any possible escape of the Japanese force.'

"B" Company, plus the Light Machine Gun platoon, would revert to control of the 1st Battalion CO [Major Henry Burgess] upon their arrival at the camp.'

"The Division Reconnaissance Platoon would complete all prior reconnaissance of the camp area and be in position to attack the enemy positions upon the opening of the first parachute at 0700.'

"My plan was to drop at a low altitude, and as close as possible outside the camp to surprise the Japanese garrison, and to avoid a concentration of enemy ground fire. The three rifle platoons would assemble on their own leaders and move directly to their objective areas to engage the enemy. The platoon leaders were briefed on their area of responsibility, and they in turn briefed their men.'

"We spent the night of 22 Feb. at Nichols Field. There was no moon."

First Lieutenant, George Skau's plan of attack.

Also, on the 22nd, Lt. George Skau met with his 31 recon platoon members, the guerrilla chiefs, and internees Ben Edwards and Freddy Zervoulakos. They had arrived over water on bancas that evening. He had previously broken down his platoon into six teams, now he attached a number of guerrillas to each team.

One team was in charge of marking the paratroop drop zone with green smoke grenades just prior to 07:00 the next morning. A second team, had the task of marking and securing the landing beach at San Antonio for the arrival of the Amtracs. The other four teams, would position themselves at different locations around the camp. He directed one team to break into the camp at the beginning of the attack and beat the exercising guards to their gun rack. Skau's squad would be responsible for destroying the guardhouse at the main entrance. [14]

Because internee Ben Edwards was familiar with the details of the camp and its perimeter defenses, Skau tasked him to accompany Sergeant Squires, six recon men, plus about twenty guerrillas to attack the guard posts on the northwest quarter of the camp. He tasked Sgt. John Fulton [the radio operator], internee Freddy Zervoulakos, and seven guerrillas to kill any escaping Japanese guards who would try to escape south of the camp to try and make it to the Japanese division.

The guerrillas assigned to the teams involved in the main assault were from the Hunters ROTC. Those assigned to mark the paratroop drop zone were the PQOG and Hukbalahaps; and for marking the amphibious force landing site were the Marking Fil-Americans.[14]

In the dark of night these teams, led by guerrillas, slowly and quietly started their trek through rice paddies, and wet marshes to their positions around the camp.

A guerrilla on one of the teams making their way to the camp was attacked by a neighbor's dog. He shot and killed the dog with his pistol. The team waited in silence and evidently that single shot did not arouse the guards' suspicions.

Chapter Fourteen

The Raid

Lt. Ringler said, "The sky was clear in the predawn, as we put on full combat equipment, then our parachutes, and loaded with our crew several weapon bundles into nine C-47s, under the command of Major Don Anderson, 75th Troop Carrier Squadron.' [28]

Paratroopers loading up for the jump.[29]

"The short flight in tight formation was unopposed by Japanese fighter planes or antiaircraft fire. As we approached the drop zone, smoke was visible. I was jumpmaster of the lead aircraft.'

"B" Company ready to jump.

Ringler was in the lead flight formation approaching the drop zone at an altitude of 400 feet. The rest were stair-stepped up to 500 feet. He saw the railroad tracks and gave the order to jump. It was 07:00 AM.

Meanwhile, back at camp, George MacDonald was cooking breakfast for the family. "Bright and early on the 23rd of February I got up to cook the rice for breakfast. I had my own recipe that called for one part rice to nine parts of water, called lugao. It would stick together well and provided us with lots of bulk. The previous night we had been sitting out under the stars with the moon shining brightly, (we could have sworn that it was blue) and thought that we had heard airplane engines. Of course we were looking for any indication that would tell us that our rescue was near.'

"Just before seven o'clock I heard airplanes. I looked to the north and saw these C-47s coming in at a very low altitude. Hollywood couldn't have provided a better setting. Nine planes flying by in tight formation and just as they got between me and the rising sun, a shape dropped out of one, then another shape and then a parachute opened, followed by chutes blossoming out all over the sky.'

"I hollered, 'paratroopers' and simultaneously with that, we could hear shots fired all over camp.'

The Filipino Guerrillas and the 11th Recon unit began attacking the guards. They had been in place the night before. [30]

"Dad had been standing up and insisted on continuing to shave but mom reached over and grabbed him and pulled him down and said, 'you didn't come this far to be shot .' We then stayed on the ground for some time, probably ten to fifteen minutes.'

Lt. Skau's two teams responsible for marking the drop zone with smoke grenades for the paratroopers and the landing zone for the Amtracs were successful in carrying out their missions.

Not all teams were in place exactly at H-hour, however this did not detract from the success of the mission. Japanese soldiers in guard towers, pill boxes and other guard posts were quickly dispatched with hand grenades, machine guns and very long and sharp bolo knives carried by the guerrillas. Lt. Skau's team was yards away from the front gate when the fighting began. They sprinted the remaining distance, took out the entrance guard post and then ran onto the compound making it to the guard's gun rack before the guards got there. The guards had been told to first put on their uniforms when they fled the calisthenics field. Evidently, it would be shameful to be caught in their loincloths.

Nurse Dorothy Still said, "We didn't know the rescue was going to happen, so we were all feeling pretty low. There was a newborn baby [Lois McCoy] and I was trying to feed her with what little powdered milk was left. The mother could hardly nurse the baby. She hadn't had enough nourishment herself. It was just about 7:00 in the morning. I had the baby in my arms when I noticed smoke signals going up'

"Then, all of a sudden, we saw a formation of aircraft coming over. As the paratroopers started jumping out, the guerrillas and soldiers around the guard houses began killing the Japanese there. Then the Amtracs came in, crashing through the sawali-covered fence near the front gate. I was holding the baby and covering her ears so that the noise wouldn't affect her. An Amtrac pulled up in front of the hospital and the American troops jumped out. Oh, we never saw anything so handsome in our lives. These fellows were in camouflage uniforms wearing a new kind of helmet, not those little tin pan things we were used to seeing. And they looked so healthy and so lively."

George continues, "The shooting subsided and we heard somebody say, 'a soldier is coming up the road.' He was beautiful. He told us to pack only what we could carry and head out to the open field up north of the barracks.'

"As we were walking toward the open field, we saw tracked vehicles lining up and instantly knew that this was what we had been hearing early in the morning. They were known as Amtracs, amphibious personnel carriers, 30 passenger capacity, with a ramp in the back, lightly armored, two machine guns, and powered by an extremely noisy aircraft engine.'

Waiting to load on the Amtracs. (note the gentleman in the foreground who wants to take his mattress with him.)

"We loaded up and in a short period of time headed out on 54 Amtracs. They had brought in a good portion of a battalion to provide perimeter defense and help in getting the prisoners loaded up.'

Amtracs loading up.

Amtracs moving out.

"The edge of the lake where they had originally landed was about a kilometer away and halfway there the Amtracs stopped abruptly, fired several bursts of machine gun fire in one direction, and then we continued. The next thing we knew we were out on the lake and they finally allowed us to look over the side. While on the land they had wanted to keep us protected from stray bullets, but now we were able to get up on the sides. It was a beautiful setting. The surface of the lake was like a mirror and here were 54 Amtracs splashing along in a line, heading for the distant shore.'

"One of the Amtracs had a little problem but they got it running again. We took some fire from Japanese gun emplacements to the east, but nothing significant - they missed us!'

"After arriving at Mamatid on the west shore of Laguna de Bay, rescue vehicles transported the internees to New Bilibid Prison. There couldn't be a better place, a prison, for safe keeping of internees, since the countryside was still not secure.'

"Once the Amtracs had successfully taken the first load of internees and deposited them on the beach at Mamatid , they returned to Los Baños and picked up the remaining prisoners, the rest of the land force that had been taken in by Amtrac and the paratroopers. This was successful, however, they had to fight a rear guard action against the Japanese that had moved into the area by the time the last Amtracs were ready to depart. As information came to light of our rescue, we were indeed fortunate that it turned out so well.'

"Our life at the New Bilibid Prison after we were rescued was frantic to begin with because everyone was hungry. The army set up field kitchens to feed the former internees resulting in chow lines longer than I have ever seen. At Santo Tomas the army had previously experienced a problem with people eating until they were sick. In this case we were starving and once started eating we didn't want to quit.   At New Bilibid Prison they restricted us to one time through the line and the   morning after our rescue, my brother John and I went thru the breakfast line and broke the rule. It had two serving areas, a main line where you got your utensils and your tray and then it split off into two lines. My brother and I had gone through once and eaten our breakfast when we noticed there was a hold up where you got your trays, so we sneaked   into the other serving line and got a second breakfast.'

Children eating real food at New Bilibid Prison.

Free at last.

The desperate physical condition of some of the former internees is evident. Men generally seemed to suffer more from hunger and malnutrition, and especially older men, than women. *(Courtesy U.S. Signal Corps)*

95

George reflects on the raid and rescue:

"This combined land, water, and air operation was unique. Each particular section of it was very important to the success of the mission.'

"First were the Amtracs bringing the backup force, out over the lake, into Los Baños.'

"Second was Airborne B Company that jumped from the nine C-47's, to the drop zone, just east of our camp.'

"Third, one of the really most important parts was the recon platoon, who, along with Filipino guerrillas, arrived overnight by native boat and forced march to surround the camp. They were in place at H hour, which was signaled by the first parachute opening. They started firing, subduing the guards, nearly all of them killed except for a few who escaped into the jungle.'

"The paratroopers did have an initial problem with prisoners who didn't want to leave their stuff and spent an inordinate amount of time gathering their belongings. Whether it was done by accident or on purpose, one of the barracks caught fire.'

Barracks Burning

"This was one way to get the people out. Anyway, then the troops set fire to the rest of them to get the people moving.'

"The prisoners didn't have a lot of belongings, but what they had was all they had in the world. Most importantly, they had survived!'

"The part of the operation that we didn't become aware of until later was the diversionary force that came down the road on the west side of the lake. The Japanese 7th division 8,000 strong, was here in the west and southwest of the camp within a three or four hour march, and they definitely had to be kept occupied. Later, when they interrogated the Japanese commanding general, he said that he had heard the noise from all these Amtracs, thought it was from tanks coming down the road and had decided it was the beginning of the American offensive. He did not find out it wasn't, until it was too late.'

"The diversionary force was extremely important and, in that force, there were two soldiers killed. Other than that the entire operation was a textbook operation. Two internees were wounded and a paratrooper sprained his ankle. The operation came off without a hitch, extracting 2147 internees safely, including a three day old baby. Nothing short of fantastic!'

Unfortunately, two Hunters' guerrillas were killed in the attack. They were Antanacio Castillo and Anselm Soler. [31]

"Today's rescues do not turn out as well. Anybody who is anyone in the paratrooper business knows of this raid. In fact even Gen. Colin Powell has acknowledged the success of this operation. The paratroopers commented afterward that they wouldn't want to do anything like that again, but if they could trade their place with anyone, they wouldn't because it was a very gratifying experience.'

511ᵗʰ Paratroopers, B Company

The day after the Los Baños Raid, General MacArthur said, "Nothing could be more satisfying to a soldier's heart than this rescue. I am deeply grateful. God was certainly with us today."

"Sometime later, I read that General MacArthur had received information that our guards had been making preparations to dispose of us, digging trenches for our graves, and placing oil barrels which could be rolled down the hillside onto the barracks to set them afire - then machine-gunning any of us who ran outside. This execution had been scheduled for that very morning of February 23, 1945. Essentially, MacArthur had stopped the war for three days in that area in order to get us out.'

"Our life at the New Bilibid Prison after we were rescued was frantic to begin with because everyone was hungry. The army set up field kitchens to feed the former internees resulting in chow lines longer than I have ever seen. At Santo Tomas the army had previously experienced a problem with people eating until they were sick. In this case we were starving and once we started eating, we didn't want to quit.'

"My brothers John and Bob were able to leave almost immediately for the U.S., but because of my illness the rest of us didn't leave for the states for several weeks. Here's what we looked like six weeks after our rescue.'

"Weight gain Mom 20 lbs, Helen 15 lbs, Dad 25 lbs and me 30 lbs.'

"We were transported by ship, the USAT Torrens, from Manila to Leyte, across to the Palau Islands, the Admiraltys, the New Hebrides and then straight to San Francisco.'

"It took about six weeks for the voyage, stopping and picking up various passengers on the way. We did have a fright somewhere south of the Hawaiian Islands when one of the engines on our ship quit and our speed was reduced to a crawl. It wasn't nice being sitting ducks, so everyone cheered when they finally got the engine fixed and we were under way again.'

"As we approached California, we were all straining our eyes, looking for the cloud-shrouded coastal mountains, and finally, there they were!! Can you imagine the thrill it gave us? Home at last!!!!! We entered San Francisco harbor after dark, the last ship in. The submarine nets were closed behind us and the vessel anchored in the harbor overnight.'

"That night, the silence was almost deafening; without engine noise, and with the excitement of being home and safe, it was hard to get to sleep.'

"The next day we disembarked and after several weeks of medical checks, etc., we traveled by train to Montana , where my mother's parents lived. We spent the summer there, but because I was sick, they kept me in bed for almost four more months.'

"When the doctor finally said I could get up and resume more or less normal activities, I had grown a foot taller! and after being at 89 pounds at my lowest ebb in February, I now weighed 150 pounds - a gain of 12 inches and 60 pounds. I was almost 15 years old.'

In her book, "Land of The Morning", my friend and fellow prisoner Jean McAnlis McMurdie wrote:

"The Los Baños rescue was not an important event in the 'big picture' of war. Many history books carry our 'story' as a brief footnote. In some history books, our rescue is not mentioned at all, for on the same day of the Los Baños rescue, February 23, 1945, the U.S. Marines raised the American flag on Mount Suribachi on Iwo Jima.'

"The battle to recapture the Island of Corregidor was raging as well, and of course, in Europe the allied spring offensive to the Rhine was starting, but, for us internees, and perhaps for our rescuers, February 23, 1945 was probably the most memorable day of our lives.'

The fate of Sadaaki Konishi.

Warrant Officer Sadaaki Konishi was captured after the war in September 1945. He went to trial in Manila for war crimes and was found guilty in January 1947 and sentenced to death by hanging. Among his convictions were,

1.) The killing of George Louis at the Los Baños Internment Camp on 28 January 1945.

2.) For aiding and abetting a policy of general starvation at the Los Baños Internment camp, thereby causing the death of four named Americans and numerous unnnamed American and civilian internees between 1 August 1944 and 23 February 1945.

He was subsequently transferred to Sugamo prison in Japan where the death sentence was carried out on 30 April 1949.[15]

Epilogue

The MacDonald family back in the United States of America.

George, Janet, Kenneth, Helen, Sibyl, Margaret, Bob, John

"After returning to the states with my parents it was decided, because of my long illness and the lack of schooling the last year when we were in Los Baños, that I would be put back a grade and so I entered my Freshman year in Missoula, Montana.'

"A year later my parents returned to the Philippines but us kids stayed behind. By this time Bob was almost out of college, Helen was in college, and John had just graduated from High School.'

< Here's George and his older brother John in 1946 after putting on much needed pounds and growing much taller than John.

"There would have been no school for me in Legaspi so if I returned with my parents I would have to be boarded out in Manila. My oldest sister, Janet, who was in the U.S. when the war broke out, had joined the Army as a nurse and there had met her husband who was a Chaplain. They offered to be my guardians while I finished high school and so I lived with them until I graduated in 1949.'

"I had worked summers for two of my aunts and their husbands, one on a dairy farm in Washington state and the other was living in California where my uncle was a crop duster. He was the one who taught me how to fly in a Piper Cub. I worked for them also at his "airport" and at The Big Orange (today it would be called a juice bar) which was quite popular.'

"The fall of 1949 found me enrolled in Lewis and Clark College in Portland, Oregon. After two years of college I was not doing nearly as well as I should have been so, in 1951, I decided to enlist in the Air Force. It was a time of the Korean War and my brother John was a pilot in the AF at that time. I figured if he could do it, I could too! I became a pilot in 1953 and served with the Air Force for thirty years. I felt I wanted to give back something to the country that had successfully given me back my life when I was just 14 and a half!"

George was selected to become a pilot in the B-58 Hustler. The aircraft that the author and Lt. Colonel "Obie" Obenauf flew in.

*George MacDonald with his B-58 crew members. Alan Bowers
(navigator), David Fossum (DSO.) Crew chief, T/Sgt. Seldenright.*

George and wife Carol

George's two sons. Steve left, Scotty right.

George closes with, "My parents retired from missionary service in 1952 and moved to Missoula where they continued to be busy with their preaching and teaching for several more years. When my father died, in 1967, his ashes were taken to the Philippines and rest in the crater of his favorite hiking place, Mt. Mayon."

Mt. Mayon, Albay, Philippines

Author's tribute to Zervoulakos, Edwards and Miles.

It is amazing that the three internees, Ben Edwards, Freddy Zervoulakos and Pete Miles not only risked their lives escaping the Los Baños prison camp but also insisted on being part of the rescue operation. Edwards and Zervoulakos were part of the recon and guerrilla attack force, while Pete Miles came in on one of the Amtracs. Miles was so exhausted from lack of sleep for three days that he had to be carried out on a stretcher when the fighting was over. Three brave men fought to save their fellow prisoners.

Author's tribute to Lieutenant George E. Skau

On 13 August 1945, six months after the Los Baños rescue, Lt. George Skau, leader of the reconnaissance platoon, was killed in a plane crash on Okinawa, Japan at the age of 30. He is buried in the 'National Memorial Cemetery of the Pacific' in Honolulu, Hawaii. Nearly 13,000 World War II Dead from the Pacific are buried here. His combined team of recon members and guerrillas played a key role, if not the most important role, in attacking the guards and freeing the civilian internees at the Los Baños Internment Camp.

We pay our respect to this soldier who was privileged to act on this mortal military stage, and in his brief time, he played his part exceedingly well.

The End

RESEARCH NOTES:

1. "MY LIFE AS A POW" by George T. MacDonald. This is a first person account by George MacDonald to tell what his life was like as a prisoner of war during the Japanese occupation of the Philippines. In his account which he shared in a PowerPoint briefing, George refers to three source documents: one being his father's diary of the war (two volumes), another is a book "That We Might Live" written by his good friend Grace Nash and the last, a book of his rescue called "The Los Baños Raid -the 11th Airborne Jumps at Dawn" by Lt. Gen L. M. Flanagan Jr. USA (ret.) who was a member of the 11th Airborne Division..

2. Unless noted otherwise, text in quotes are attributed to George MacDonald in his own words.

3. Japan's Strategy In The Pacific And Southeast Asia,
https://www.britannica.com/topic/Pacific-War

4. History of the University of the Philippines Los Baños (UPLB.)
https://web.archive.org/web/20090720100734/http://www.old.uplb.edu.ph/about/uplb-history

5. Camp map and barracks drawings were done by internee Leo Stancliff.

6. The Navy Department Library, Oral Histories - U.S. Navy Nurse Prisoner of War in the Philippines, 1942-1945, Recollections of LT Dorothy Still Danner, NC, USN, captured by the Japanese in Manila and imprisoned at Santo Thomas and Los Baños in the Philippines, Adapted from: "Dorothy Still Danner: Reminiscences of a Nurse POW." Navy Medicine 83, no. 3 (May-June 1992): 36-40 – *U.S. Navy photo.*

7. Appendix A. of "The Los Baños Raid -the 11th Airborne Jumps at Dawn" 1986 by Lt. Gen E. M. Flanagan Jr. USA (ret.)

8. From Sister Kreuger's Obituary March 9, 1989

9. "That We Might Live" by Grace Nash, 1984

10. From the website http://ithascome.bravehost.com/index.html This site was built to honor the memory of Herman Knight Beaber. It also contains recollections of other Los Baños Internees.

11. "75 years later, Montanans remember World War II days of triumph", by Kim Briggeman, Feb 21, 2020, Missoulian newspaper article. *Excerpts about John MacDonald's Los Baños life.*

12. Sourced from Email correspondence between Lois McCoy Bourinskie and the author in March 2020.

13. P-38-Lightning-pursuit, Lockheed-Aircraft-Corporation, Britannica.com

14. "Angels at Dawn - The Los Baños Raid",1999, by Lt. Gen. Edward M. Flanagan Jr. USA (Ret.)

15. "Rescue at Los Baños: The Most Daring Prison Camp Raid of World War II", by Bruce Henderson, 2015

16. "MAJOR JAY D. VANDERPOOL - Advisor to the Philippine Guerrillas" by Michael E. Krivdo, PhD, As it appeared in The U.S. Army Special Operations Command (USASOC) History Office for the Army Special Operations Forces. From Veritas, Vol. 9, No. 1, 2013, https://arsof-history.org/articles/v9n1_vanderpool_page_1.html

17. USAMHI, Senior Officers Oral History Program: Project 83-12:Jay D. Vanderpool, Colonel, USA (Ret.), Project 83-12 [Carlisle, 1983], pp. 84-119; Ltr, Vanderpool to Commanding General, Ryukus Command, 5 Aug 47, Jay D. Vanderpool Papers, USAMHI.

18. The Palawan Massacre, 14 Dec 1944, from "American POWs of Japan" - a research project of Asia Policy Point, a Washington, DC-based nonprofit that studies the US policy relationship with Japan and Northeast Asia. The project aims to educate Americans on the history of the POW experience both during and after World War II and its effect on the US-Japan alliance.

http://americanpowsofjapan.blogspot.com/2011/12/palawan-massacre-december-14-1944.html

19. "American Prisoners of War: Massacre at Palawan" from HistoryNet and based on an article written by V. Dennis Wrynn, originally appeared in the November 1997 issue of *World War II* magazine. https://www.historynet.com/american-prisoners-of-war-massacre-at-palawan.htm

20. Reports of General MacArthur, The Campaigns of MacArthur In the Pacific, Volume 1 (Chapter 8, "The Leyte Operation" and Chapter 9, "The Mindoro and Luzon Opeation" https://history.army.mil/books/wwii/macarthur%20reports/macarthur%20v1/ch08.htm https://history.army.mil/books/wwii/MacArthur%20Reports/MacArthur%20V1/ch09.htm#b5

21. Terror & Triumph at Lingayen Gulf, an article by James M. Scott, October 2018 Naval History Magazine Volume 32, Number 5. Mr. Scott is the author of Target Tokyo (W. W. Norton, 2015), which was a 2016 Pulitzer Prize finalist for history. His latest book, from which this article is adapted, is Rampage: MacArthur, Yamashita, and the Battle of Manila (W. W. Norton, 2018).

22. Rampage: MacArthur, Yamashita, and the Battle of Manila, by James M. Scott

23. Kamikaze attack photo appeared on U.S. Naval Institute Web Page https://www.usni.org/magazines/naval-history-magazine/2018/october/terror-triumph-lingayen-gulf

24. "The Gallant Buccaneer of Los Baños" by Grace Nash, Reader's Digest, Feb 1959.

25. This map of the Los Baños camp was the best and most complete one the author was able to find. It was from "Combat Notes Number 7. Assistant Chief of Staff, G3, Headquarters, 6th Army, May 1945. It was annotated with additional information by the author.

26. The most probable route for the C-47s was a direct flight to the southern tip of Talim Island and then straight to the Drop Zone. As a navigator for thirteen years and based on the limited navigation equipment for C-47s at the time, it is how the author would have planned the flight, rather than trying to navigate a direct course to the drop zone.

27. Source for two U.S. soldier fatalities https://military.wikia.org/wiki/Raid_on_Los_Ba%C3%B1os#Historical_significance

28. "THE LOS BAÑOS RAID", by John M. Ringler, as it appeared in "WINDS ALOFT" a Quarterly publication of the 511th Parachute Infantry Association. Photo curtesy 'of sticksandstones'

29. Paratroopers of the 511th Parachute Infantry Regiment prepare for their combat jump on Tagaytay Ridge, 20 days before they jump on Los Baños. National Archives, U.S. Army Signal Corps.

30. Public domain photo of a painting. Clearly shown in the painting is a guerrilla armed with a bolo knife divesting a Japanese sentry of his rifle. Crouched behind the foliage and clutching U.S. issued .30 caliber M1903 series rifles, are other members of the force who wait to assist the 11th Airborne force landing in front of the camp.

31. Rottman, G.L., 2010, The Los Baños Prison Camp Raid, Oxford: Osprey Publishing Ltd.

32. From the Website 'Philippine Internment, World War II in the Philippine http://philippineinternment.com/?

33. Records of the Office of Provost Marshal General, American Pow Information Bureau Records Brnch, General Subject File, 1942-46, Archive File 615-1, "CENSUS LIST. CIVILIAN INTERNMENT CAMP No. 2 [Los Baños] , As of December 25th 1944, American Nationals This record is important for genealogical research because it lists the Name, Sex, Age, and Occupation of all Americans on the list. The author has chosen not to show sex and occupation for American internees in Appendix D due to space limitations, however ages are shown.

34. Lois McCoy's parents' marriage: Mildred Alene Palmer and Oscar Gervius "Mac" McCoy, Apr. 18, 1944 Los Baños Internment Camp from "Love and Marriage" section of http://philippineinternment.com/?page_id=1172
Oscar was 35 and Mildred was 27 at the time of their marriage.

35. CATALYST FOR ACTION, The Palawan Massacre, by Michael E. Krivdo, PhD, WWII, PHILIPPINES, LEGACY, From Veritas, Vol. 14, No. 1, 2018

36. The Heroes of Palawan – How Survivors of a Japanese Massacre Lived to Tell the Tale of Atrocities in the Philippines, by Stephen L. Moore, MilitaryHistoryNow.com, 2 December, 2016

37. HON. TJ COX OF CALIFORNIA, IN THE HOUSE OF REPRESENTATIVES, Monday, December 16, 2019, Congressional Record Vol. 165, No. 203

38. Type 97 (B5N1) "Kate" Carrier Attack Bombers flying from aircraft carrier Ryujo are shown flying near Mayon Volcano on their way to attack Legaspi, southeast of Luzon, Philippines. Captain Masayuki Yamagami is in command. 12 December 1941 ("Album of a Navy Captain" via Egoo.net).

39. Last Man Out - Glenn McDole, USMC, Survivor of the Palawan Massacre in World War II, by Bob Wilbanks

40. Full text of "CMH Pub 13-3 Reports of General MacArthur: Volume I, The Campaigns of MacArthur in the Pacific"
https://archive.org/stream/ReportsOfGeneralMacarthurTheCampaigns/ReportsOfGeneralMac arthurTheCampaigns_djvu.txt

Other Resources

Bataan Death March, by History.com Editors. https://www.history.com/topics/world-war-ii/bataan-death-march

Rescue at Dawn: The Los Baños Raid. Documentary | TV Movie, 15 February 2004

The Case of General Yamashita a Memorandum by Courtney Whitney, Brigadier General, U.S. Army, Chief, Government Section. dated 22 Nov 1949

Shadows in the Jungle, by Larry Alexander, names of the two guerrillas that were killed. Also on page 313 Lois Bourinskie is mentioned as the "Baby" Lois McCoy, "who was carried out of Los Baños at age three days. She graduated from the Providence College of Nursing in Oakland, California, in 1966 and worked at Southwest Washington Medical Center in Vancouver Washington, as a registered nurse, Widowed more than twenty years ago, she still lives there, painting watercolors and acrylics."

"The Los Baños Raid -the 11th Airborne Jumps at Dawn" 1986 by Lt. Gen E. M. Flanagan Jr. USA (ret.)

"General MacArthur returns to the Philippines" Author, History.com Editors https://www.history.com/this-day-in-history/macarthur-returns

"MacArthur's Return to the Philippines" Author: Carole D. Bos, J.D. The details of what happened on the 20th of October are from *Reports of General MacArthur, The Campaigns of MacArthur in the Pacific*, Volume 1 (Chapter 8, "The Leyte Operation"): https://www.awesomestories.com/asset/view/MacArthur-s-Return-to-the-Philippines

Desperate Los Baños Raid By Christopher Miskimon https://warfarehistorynetwork.com/2020/04/03/desperate-los-banos-raid/

1LT George E. Skau, born 22 Nov 1914, died `13 Aug 1945 (aged 30) He is buried in the National Memorial Cemetery of the Pacific, Honolulu, Hawaii. His grave shows that he entered the service from Connecticut. Nearly 13,000 World War II Dead from the Pacific are buried here. Photo added by Jeff Hall – cropped and straightened by the author.

"Frank Buckles, Last World War I Doughboy, Is Dead at 110" New York Times article by Richard Goldstein, •   Feb. 28, 2011

"Remembering a World War II Death Trap — and a Miraculous Rescue" by CHRISTINE SNYDER, . FEB. 23, 2015

From the journal of Sofia G. Tidon who was a 14-year-old freshman at the University of the Philippines Rural High School, located on the Los Baños campus. She writes ""The Hukbalahap (Hukbo ng Bayan Laban sa Hapon) was assigned to secure the jump site in the vicinity of the railroad crossing and Pili Drive. The 25th Red Lions PQOG under the command of Colonel Price [nom de guerre of Gen. Romeo Espino] would secure the landing [site] of the amphibians in Mayundon and set up blocking forces." By: Danielle Elisha F. Ching - @inquirerdotnet, Philippine Daily Inquirer / 06:52 PM May 06, 2013

Full text of war crimes
https://archive.org/stream/USMilitaryCommissionRecordsMicrofilm/%28Reel%2087%29%20US%20military%20trial%20reports%20197-203_djvu.txt

30 minute movie los Baños rescue https://www.youtube.com/watch?v=JOb2XoMyCe4

Manila Nostalgia – 70th Anniversary los Baños rescue – great photos
http://www.lougopal.com/manila/?p=2844

Hunters ROTC – great site   http://adroth.ph/Hunters/Stories/whowerethey.htm

Freedom at dawn – about the Hunters   http://www.paete.org/literary/freedom/part4.htm

American POWs of Japan is a research project of Asia Policy Point, a Washington, DC-based nonprofit that studies the US policy relationship with Japan and Northeast Asia. The project aims to educate Americans on the history of the POW experience both during and after World War II and its effect on the US-Japan alliance.

George Holt, Jr.

Heroes I've Known

Part 2.

James "Obie" Obenauf

One Man's Courage – Two Lives Saved

113

We are about to embark on a story that will continue to be told in the annals of Military history, for years to come. It is the story of First Lieutenant James "Obie" Obenauf, a copilot who found himself flying a B-47 bomber aircraft from the back seat, after his pilot and navigator had bailed out.

Chapter One

The Mission

28 April 1958, 7:55 PM:

This was a special mission for Major Graves' crew. The bomb wing was anticipating a visit from the 3908th Strategic Evaluation Group. The 3908th was a Strategic Air Command select unit that visited bomber bases to evaluate the readiness of aircrews to perform their wartime mission. They were especially critical in their assessments of those crews having the responsibility of testing all other crews within the wing. Graves' crew was one of those so-called wing standardization crews.

Major Joe Maxwell was on this flight to prepare the navigator Lt. John Cobb to be at his best when being evaluated by the 3908th. As the wing's chief navigation instructor, he would observe, evaluate, and recommend refinements to Cobb's technique for making simulated bomb runs.

Obie the copilot and relative newcomer to B-47s was fortunate to be chosen to fly with Graves and Cobb. He learned a lot from Graves on how to fly this bomber and except for landings, which were virtually impossible from the back sea, he felt confident in all other aspects of flight. He and Cobb, the navigator, worked well together on the navigation and bombing portions of their missions.

Obie climbs aboard as the crew gets ready to start engines.

Obie waiting for the pilot to take his seat up front.

Engines started. Before taxi checklists completed. Binbrock 16 taxis to the end of the runway and awaits clearance for takeoff.

"Binbrock 16 this is Dyess tower. You're cleared for takeoff."

Binbrock 16 was the call sign for the B-47 bomber about to take off that evening from Dyess Air Force Base in Abilene Texas. The three man crew would be on a Strategic Air Command training mission to include, celestial navigation, air refueling and high altitude simulated bomb runs. Also on board was an instructor navigator, evaluating the performance of the crew's navigator.

117

With his feet firmly on the brakes the pilot, Major Jim Graves advanced the throttles to full power. Watching his engine instruments unwind he could feel the vibration and hear the high pitched whine of the six jet engines as they wound up to full power.

"Dyess tower, this is Binbrock 16, releasing brakes and rolling."

"Binbrock 16, Roger, you're cleared for a climb on course to flight level 28,000 ft."

"Navigator to Pilot, take up a heading of three, three zero degrees to Amarillo.'

The crew planned to spend about an hour doing simulated bomb runs on targets in Amarillo. Obie could hear Cobb and Maxwell chatting over the interphone. [13]

Maxwell, "Nav, in case you lose your radar crosshairs, how would you make a manual bomb release on the target."

Cobb, "I'd set the cursor to my best known crosswind, and keep the target lined up under the cursor, by giving the pilot small heading corrections."

Maxwell, "That's good, but how would you determine your groundspeed. That's the most important factor to ensure a successful bomb drop?"

Cobb, "I would start my stop watch when the target hit the 20 mile range marker and stop it when it hit the ten. Then compute the groundspeed based on how long it took to travel those ten miles."

Maxwell, "Yes, and I see you have your other stop watch to start at the same time the target crossed the ten mile range marker. What next"

Cobb, "I'd go into my bombing tables to determine the time to release from the ten mile marker."

Maxwell, "I don't think the evaluator would ask you to make a manual release, but he could ask those same types of questions, so be prepared."

Cobb had completed his third and last run on Amarillo. He called Graves on interphone, "Pilot, this is Nav, climb to 34,000 feet for the start of the celestial navigation leg."

"Obie after this last bomb run, I'll need you to use the sextant to shoot some stars on our celestial leg to Denver."

"Roger Nav, I'll be ready."

The copilot, Lieutenant James "Obie" Obenauf was getting ready to use the bubble sextant to 'shoot the stars' to assist navigator/bombardier, Lieutenant John Cobb.

Cobb began computing approximate azimuth and elevation information for three stars that would give him a good celestial fix. He passed this info to Obie.

When ready, Obie would insert the sextant up and into a round, trap door opening in the canopy. When he found one of the stars, he would start a timer while keeping the star centered in his eyepiece. The elevation of the star would be averaged over two minutes and he would transmit this info back to Cobb. After three stars were shot the nav would plot a three star fix on his navigation map.

Later modifications to B-47s installed a sextant port in the navigator's station, allowing the nav to shoot stars on his own. But like Obie and other copilots of the early B-47 era, they learned a lot about how to locate and identify stars most suitable for navigation. To this day they would no doubt be able to look up into the night sky and point out stars like Altares, Altair, Arcturus, Capella, Spica and Vega to name a few.

Major Maxwell was pleased with the performance of Cobb and Obie. "Good team work" he thought.

The pilot, Major Jim Graves, also known as the Aircraft Commander had been monitoring his instruments and didn't like what he saw on engine number three.

"Crew, it looks like we're losing oil pressure on number 3. I'm advancing the throttle on that engine . . . OK, we're back within limits, but I may have to shut down that engine if this keeps up. Obie, keep an eye on that for me, will you?"

"Roger, wilco."

Except for takeoff, landing, and air refueling these long 8 hour missions could be somewhat boring for Graves. He started reminiscing about his time he flew B-17s over Germany during World War II. He remembered a flight over Dresden when he saw a

B-17 ahead of him that had been hit. He heard the pilot yell, "Bail out! Bail Out! Bail Out!" but no one bailed out and he saw the aircraft burst into flames and go down.[8]

"Enough of that," he thought. He opened his flight lunch and began eating some fried chicken.

Except for the ever present vibrations and the low whine of the engines, and the occasional chat between Cobb and Maxell, it was relatively quiet in the aircraft. Obie was checking the fuel status and everything looked fine.

Major Maxwell had taken off his cumbersome chest pack parachute and was sitting in the crawlway on a folding metal chair. He began eating a chicken drumstick from his flight lunch. Little did the crew know what this beast of an airplane had in store for them.

Chapter Two
The Aircraft

The B-47 Stratojet:

B-47 displayed at Grissom Air Museum in Indiana

The Boeing B-47 was the country's first swept-wing multiengine bomber. In the 1950s it represented a milestone in aviation history and a revolution in aircraft design. Early wind tunnel tests of straight-wing jet aircraft indicated that the straight wing did not use the full potential of jet-engine power. The B-47 with its slender 35-degree swept-back wings allowed much faster airspeeds and this graceful jet soon started breaking speed and distance records. In 1949, it crossed the United States in under four hours at an average 608 mph. The B-47 needed defensive armament only in the rear because no fighter was fast enough to attack from any other angle. [6]

This medium bomber became the foundation of the Air Force's newly created Strategic Air Command (SAC), and over 2,000 B-47s in all variants were built. SAC deployed a total of 27 B-47 wings. Each wing had 60 aircraft assigned. By 1956, SAC had over 1200 combat-ready B-47 crews assigned to fly these aircraft.

Obie's cockpit position is shown as #3. The Navigator's position #1 is just above and forward of the radome which hosts the radar antenna #26. Normal entry and exit to the aircraft is through the opening at #25.

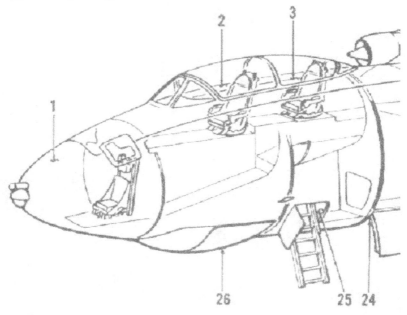

There was no entry through the canopy, however it could remain partially open during engine start, especially on a hot day.

The copilot sat behind the pilot. This position affords almost no forward visibility which is critical for a successful landing.

The pilot's cockpit.

This is a cutaway view of the catwalk to the navigator's station.

When the navigator/ bombardier was on a bomb run, he would acquire the target on radar and then at a certain distance from the target he would ask the Aircraft Commander for second station. In second station he could control the aircraft's heading with the use of his tracking handle, shown in the next photo, in white.

Radar Bomb Scoring (RBS) sites scored bomb runs by acquiring the inbound aircraft on radar. The aircraft's track was drawn in ink on a large horizontal white board. This track was based on the aircraft's ground speed and true course. Ten seconds before bomb release the aircraft would transmit a constant tone. At simulated bomb release the tone stops and the pen on the plotting board lifts up. At that point, the RBS site operators would extend the track based on the time of fall for the bomb type and the best-known wind data. Altogether, this determined how close the bomb would have come to the target.

The instructor navigator on this flight, Major Joseph Maxwell, would be positioned just behind the navigator standing or sitting in the crawlway on a folding metal chair. If forced to bail out, he would normally exit through the entrance hatch #25.

The B-47 had a good radar and bomb/nav system. However, with vacuum tube technology, reliability was not that great. Navigator/bombardiers were trained to perform in-flight maintenance and they often had to swap out line replaceable units (LRUs) to keep the Radar and Navigation system up and running.

The author was a Navigator/Bombardier in this airplane from 1960 to 1966. He accumulated more than 2,500 hours while stationed at Pease Air Force Base, Portsmouth, New Hampshire. The author notes, "I wore a very heavy back pack parachute and my map table was off to my right. It was quite uncomfortable to be constantly turning from the radar scope to the map table to plot positions or to compute celestial data. My back would ache after a seven to eight-hour mission."

Before drogue parachutes were installed on nuclear bombs, bomber aircraft were at risk of being blown out of the sky from the impact of a nuclear blast. B-47, crews trained in "pop-up" bombing attacks by coming in at low-level and then climbing rapidly on nearing the target. At the proper altitude, they would release a nuclear weapon (simulated for training missions) into an arc and then roll away to depart the target area and hopefully escape the nuclear blast.

Here's another more stressful maneuver that the B-47 practiced to safely escape a nuclear blast. Marshall Michel describes it best in the 2003 issue of Air & Space Magazine. [12]

"At an air force firepower demonstration held at Eglin Air Force Base in Florida on May 7, 1957, a silvery swept-wing Boeing B-47 Stratojet bomber roared in low at 500 mph before a crowd of more than 3,000 people. The six-jet bomber tore past the front of the reviewing stand, which was filled with high-ranking military officers and 11 state governors, then pulled up into a steep climb and continued up, up, until it was almost standing on its tail. The bomb bay doors snapped open and an orange practice bomb, trailing smoke from a pyrotechnic device in its tail, arced up and away from the bomber.'

"The audience watched transfixed as the B-47 continued until it was upside down at the top of a half loop. Then, still inverted, it started down the back side of the loop, rolled right side up, and dove away in the direction from which it had come. This was the first public demonstration of a B-47 performing a new mode of nuclear weapons delivery that had been developed far from public view five years earlier. Not just the B-47 but a long list of tactical fighter-bombers would employ the startling new maneuver, which was called toss bombing." [47.]

This maneuver was discontinued when it was feared that the high 'G' forces on the wings and longitudinal body of the B-47 would cause irreparable damage over time.

The B-47 also had the capability to take off from short runways using attachable external rockets that were jettisoned when spent.

Flying the aircraft at approach and landing speeds was demanding because the engines were slow to accelerate. A drogue parachute was used to allow approach and landings to be made with the engines still carrying enough power to enable rapid throttle movement. After landing, a 32-foot brake chute and anti-skid brakes stopped the aircraft.

Drogue parachute deployed prior to landing.

The B-47 was not a forgiving aircraft. Unlike straight wing aircraft, you had to stay ahead of it. There was little room for error. Swept wing aircraft also required pilots to unlearn what heretofore had been normal responses to emergency situations with straight wing aircraft.

For example in the B-47, the loss of an outboard engine on takeoff required immediate opposite rudder and not the use of the control wheel yoke. Losing the outboard engine caused the plane to yaw, or turn, into the dead engine. With the B-47's swept wings, this caused the wing with the dead engine to lose lift and the other wing to gain lift, causing a roll into the dead engine. If the wheel yoke was used to turn the aircraft in the opposite direction it created additional drag on the wing and loss of control soon followed. A number of these accidents occurred with the B-47 cartwheeling and exploding off the end of the runway.

This condition was also experienced in the B-58. I documented this in my book, "The B-58 Blunder – How the U.S. Abandoned its Best Strategic Bomber" I wrote that a Convair test pilot and engineer were killed when a B-58 lost an outboard engine while flying at Mach 2. This was a test flight to see if the pilot could control adverse yaw using only the B-58's control stick and without using rudders. For normal operation, the B-58 had a yaw damper system that was supposed to automatically control adverse yaw by applying opposite rudder to stop the yawing motion.

In this test, the aircraft was a well instrumented test bed with recording devices taking up the entire space in the Navigator's position. The test engineer, occupied the DSO's position.

The test began at Mach 2 at 35,000 feet, with all four engines in full afterburner and with the pilot's feet on the floor. He flipped a switch that instantly failed the right outboard engine. The aircraft side-slipped in the direction of the lost engine and immediately disintegrated. Convair test pilot Ray Fitzgerald and flight test engineer Don Siedhof, the only two crewmembers aboard, were killed instantly. Their bodies were later found, still strapped in their ejection seats.

The test was built around a worse-case scenario. For one, it was conducted at 35,000 feet instead of 55,000 feet. At 35,000 feet the air is more than twice as dense as the air found at 55,000 feet, the B-58's normal altitude for supersonic flight. Therefore, the drag on a failed engine and airframe would be much greater when experiencing an adverse yaw condition. Secondly, the aircraft was put in a relatively unstable condition by transferring fuel to the aft tank, creating an aft center of gravity (CG.) Thirdly, the test had been previously conducted at Mach 1.6 with no adverse effects, and subsequent tests were supposed to be run in a stair-step approach to Mach 2 by increasing the Mach number in 10% increments. But, Convair decided to skip those incremental steps and go directly to the Mach 2 test.

Left unchecked, when an aircraft experiences an adverse yaw condition, (in this case the loss of an engine – on the right side) it starts a lateral turn/slip toward that engine. In doing so, it also starts a rolling motion. This rolling motion is much more pronounced in swept wing aircraft like the B-58, and B-47. In this example, the left wing gains lift and the right wing loses lift due to the left wing becoming less-swept than the right wing, in reference to the relative wind, causing the aircraft to roll to the right.

So, when Fitzgerald, the test pilot, felt that first yawing motion, coupled with the rolling motion, it's assumed he forced the control stick hard left. But in doing so he created more drag on the right side of the aircraft as the B-58's huge elevons (acting as ailerons) were forced down into the airstream. This additional drag on the right side accelerated the turning and rolling of the aircraft to the right until breakup occurred.

Getting back to B-47 accidents, here's what Walter J. Boyne wrote about the B-47s accident history. [2] Boyne was a former B-47 pilot.

"Everyone, including pilots' families, knew that this aircraft, while magnificent, was also very unforgiving. The B-47's cutting-edge design pushed the boundaries of both aerodynamics and pilot experience. Yet for young pilots eager to enter the Jet Age, knowing that the aircraft could be difficult heightened the pleasure of flying it.'

"When the B-47 was introduced, it was simply too radical in its aerodynamics and in its demands for unrelentingly professional airmanship. The new United States Air Force was still operating under World War II attitudes. New swept-wing jets demanded much higher standards, yet far too little emphasis was placed on safety and rigorous training. Accident rates and fatalities skyrocketed.'

"In 1957 alone, there were 28 fatal accidents and 63 deaths. The common denominator of the accidents was that the circumstances were routine, familiar. In case after case, there was some minor but fatal human error. In a fast instrument let-down, the pilot might turn the wrong way and run into a mountain. Misreading an altimeter led to a smoking hole in the ground. A 15-second lapse of attention in a descending turn could let airspeed build so fast that a safe recovery was impossible. In earlier, more forgiving aircraft, these mistakes might have been survivable, but in the B-47, they were disastrous. Some accidents were caused by maintenance errors, but these were less common. All too often the accident investigation ended with the heartless but accurate phrase "pilot error."

With this back drop, Obie came to B-47s directly after pilot training and had flown only 220 hours in the B-47 prior to this mission on 28 April 1958.

Chapter Three

The Aircrew

This was a top notch aircrew. They were chosen by their wing commander in 1957, to participate in the Strategic Air Command's bombing competition. This was a yearly event that pitted the best bomber crews from all over the U.S. against each other in bombing and navigation trials.

Along with Obie, the rest of the aircrew on that ill-fated mission on 28 April 1958, was the pilot, Major James Graves, the navigator/ bombardier Lieutenant John Cobb and Joe Maxwell an instructor navigator who was evaluating the performance of Cobb, the navigator. [8]

Major James Graves joined the Air Corps in 1942 at the age of eighteen. Like Obie, Jim got his commission and wings through the Aviation Cadet program.

After the war, Graves left the service for a while but rejoined to fly C-54s carrying supplies into Berlin during the Berlin Airlift. He also saw service during the Korean War and had bombed targets in North Korea.[8] Obie could not have been more fortunate to be paired up with this pilot who had already flown thousands of combat hours in two wars.

Lieutenant John Cobb

Lt. Cobb was from Elko Nevada. His father died when John was two years old so he spent most of his growing up years living with his grandparents. John's Uncle Archie had a strong influence on John and he was probably the one who instilled in John a desire to fly. Archie was in World War Two and flew B-17s. He wrote many letters to John from England describing his exploits. Cobb's navigation skills were exemplary.

Major Joe Maxwell

On this mission, Major Maxwell had been in the Air Force for 15 years. He and his wife Doe Maxwell had five young children at the time Gary, 8, John, 7, Tim, 5, Joe, 2 and a baby just 10 months old.

Joe's father was in the Navy and spent much time at sea while Joe was growing up. His father retired from the Navy in 1934, during the great depression, so Joe had to help out as best he could, earning extra money at odd jobs – mowing lawns, working as a caddy on a golf course, a paper route, and then as a server in an ice cream parlor. In 1940 his Mom and Dad divorced, and Joe worked even harder at any jobs where he could find work. He graduated from high school in 1942 in the midst of the Second World War and when he was old enough, he joined the Army Air Corps.

He was sent to the University of Alabama to take courses in navigation and by the time the war ended he had earned his navigator wings and a commission as a 2nd Lieutenant.

Joe married Doe while he was at Carswell Air Force Base, then spent a tour in Japan. When he returned, he was assigned as a navigator on the B-36 bomber.

The B-36 was a huge aircraft – big enough where a maintenance technician could stand up inside one of the wings.

The day before Joe was to take off on this aircraft's maiden flight, he came down with a toothache and the base doctor grounded him. That aircraft crashed on takeoff the next day killing all four crew members in the same compartment Joe would have been in.

Chapter Four
James "Obie" Obenauf

The odyssey that brought Lt. Obenauf to be in the backseat of this powerful B-47 aircraft began from his roots as a member of a large farming family. Obie, the youngest of nine children, was born on a farm in Mundelein, Illinois. Here he is at the age of six, next to his father.

The Obenauf name is an old German name meaning 'uppermost' or 'up on top.'

Coming out of the great depression during the 1930s, Obie along with his siblings, all had farm chores to do. From early morn till evening there was milking, planting, hoeing, wood chopping, collecting eggs, and mucking out the horse and cow stalls.

In his spare time he played baseball and had a passion for building and flying model airplanes. While in High School he was able to take flying lessons with money he made by helping a farm neighbor with his crops.

Having no desire to go to college after High School and no desire to be drafted, Obie joined the Air Force in 1954. Hoping to become a pilot, he was disappointed to find out that he needed a college degree to apply for pilot training. However, he discovered an alternative for gaining his wings.

The Aviation Cadet program was a long standing program utilized to meet the demand for additional pilots and navigators. It allowed qualified enlisted airmen to enter this program and after a year of combined officer training and flight training, they received their wings and commission.

The author entered the program about the same time as Obie. I received my navigator wings and 2nd Lieutenant commission in February 1956.

Obie took his flight training at Bainbridge Air Base, Georgia. Civilian pilots were the instructors. He started out in the PA-18 .

PA-18

He then graduated to the T-6 Texan.

After Bainbridge Obie was transferred to Williams Air Force Base where he continued his training in the T-28 and the T-33.

North American T-28

The Lockheed T-33 Jet Trainer

Obie received his wings and was commissioned as a 2nd Lieutenant in 1956. He then was assigned to B-47s at Dyess AFB in Abilene Texas.

As soon as he got to Dyess, Obie took leave and went to Chicago to marry Pat Connors. He and Pat had dated on and off ever since their blind date around the ages of 15.

Pat lived in Chicago but she and her parents vacationed often around the Mundelein, Illinois area. While Pat was at home in Chicago, Obie would occasionally drive the 30 miles to meet her.

After four years of courtship and when Obie was 19, he asked Pat to marry him after he got his commission and wings, and of course she agreed.

Chapter Five

Explosion and Fire

Flying at 34,000 feet, the crew had passed Amarillo, Texas, heading for Denver, Colorado. The oil pressure on engine #3, had been stabilized for some time now.

Then it hit like a sledge hammer, the aircraft lurched and vibrated – something was seriously wrong. Cobb yelled on the intercom "What was that?" No one answered.

Obie remembers, "There was a huge explosion . . . you could definitely hear it. The aircraft shuddered and rocked and the right wing appeared to be engulfed in flames. It was shooting flames and sparks 30 to 40 feet in every direction.'

Obie yelled on intercom "We're on fire!"

Major Graves yelled over interphone, "Bail out. Bail out. Bail out."

Obie felt the wind in his face as the pilot jettisoned the airplane's canopy.

Obie recalls, "The first man I know of that left the aircraft was the navigator … I tried to eject, but my ejection seat failed. I went all the way through the ejection sequence. The control column had stowed, the seat had bottomed, the canopy flew off. I raised my ejection handles and squeezed the triggers – nothing happened. I put the handles down, raised them again, and squeezed the triggers – nothing."

Cobb had turned his seat forward, pulled his feet in and then pulled the D ring between his legs and he was blown downward into the airstream by an explosive charge behind his seat. There was an immediate rush of sub-freezing air that entered the aircraft. It picked up dirt and debris as it streamed back and up through the canopy opening, temporarily blinding Obie.

Obie said, "Approximately at the time the navigator, Lieutenant Cobb, bailed out, Major Maxwell was already up near the navigator. He was blown back head first and hit somewhere near my position. Immediately after this, he seemed to shake his head and went forward. I assumed he was all right.'

"Since I could not eject, I immediately tried to get out of my seat. I had an awful lot of trouble because my survival kit kept catching on everything. I got down to the escape hatch, pulled the master lever but the pressure door did not operate . . . helmet bags, flight lunches, and other things were caught in there. I was then going up to the navigator's hatch to bail out when I noticed that Major Maxwell was now lying in the aisle. I assumed he was hypoxic, so I immediately climbed back up in the seat and checked on the fire. If it was too bad, I was going over the side. But I thought if there was half a chance of going on, I would stay with the aircraft.'

"First, I had to unstow the control column. I tried pulling it back but it wouldn't budge. I tried again with all my strength and was now able to break it free.'

Even though both pilots' control columns had been stowed automatically when they went through their ejection procedure, the airplane remained on autopilot. However, if Obie had not been able to break the spring on the control column and reengage it, he would not have been able to fly the airplane.

"The fire seemed under control. It was confined to No. 6 engine, so I actuated the throttle to cut off and it did turn the fire down to a bright glow all over the engine.'

"I immediately started a descent . . . to get to a lower altitude so that Major Maxwell would wake up and bail out and I could get out.'

At this time, aside from the frigid air, both Obie and Major Maxwell were in danger of losing consciousness due to hypoxia. Hypoxia is a silent killer because it hits you without warning and you pass out without ever realizing you're in trouble. At altitudes above 25,000 feet there is less than 1/3 the amount of oxygen in the air.

The author remembers his experience in the Air Force's altitude chamber when air in the chamber was pumped out to simulate an altitude of 27, 000 feet. We were told to remove our oxygen masks. Breathing remained normal. We were asked to do simple chores like writing our name and address on a piece of paper. After three or four minutes everything felt fine – no heavy breathing – some tingling in the fingers – a somewhat euphoric feeling – but my handwriting was getting large, unreadable, and running off the page. But I thought I was doing fine. At this point we were told to put our oxygen masks back on and some had to be helped with this simple chore.

Obie, realizing he could not last long without oxygen made the right decision to climb back into his seat connect to oxygen and put the airplane in a steep dive to an altitude where the oxygen levels were more near normal.

"At approximately 11,000 feet, my oxygen cut out and I was unable to read the liters in the converters because of dust in my eyes and wind blast. I could not see my instruments accurately. I was mostly flying by feel. I leveled off about 10,000 feet.'

"Major Maxwell started shaking his head and I started hitting him on the head and yelling at him 'Bail out, bail out.' I screamed at him 'BAIL OUT.' Then I realized, he didn't have his parachute.'

"For at least 20 minutes, I tried to talk him into finding his parachute and bailing out. He could hear me but couldn't answer me because we had lost interphone connection. He just grabbed my leg and looked up at me, as if to say 'Don't leave me.' He looked groggy as if he was about to pass out'

"Finally, I checked the engine and there was no more red glow.'

"I had been giving maydays over the radio but I realized that my interphone cord had been disconnected, so apparently, I was a little hypoxic myself. I connected my interphone cord and immediately gave a mayday, my position, and that the other crew-members had bailed out.'

"Altus DF [Direction Finding] picked up my mayday. Also, another B-47, Eyelash 32 was in the air and he was telling people on the ground exactly what I could do from the back seat. Ground was asking me to squawk mayday, etc., and he convinced them that I couldn't do it from the back seat.'

"Decision . . . I kept descending until I got down to 5500 feet and Altus gave me a heading for Dyess Air Force Base. I tried to maintain that heading but couldn't see the directional indicator. I had no idea what my heading was and so I realized more or less this was a gyro out steer which worked out fairly well until Fat Chance GCI [Ground Control Intercept] picked me up; but he was coming in so garbled I was unable to read most of his transmissions. Finally, Dyess DF and Reese DF got me into the station.'

With an open hole under the aircraft, up front where the navigator had bailed out and with the pilot's canopy gone, this B-47 was no longer a streamlined aerodynamic platform. There was buffeting and bouncing which commanded Obie's constant attention all the way back to Dyess.

And now he was getting ready to land this beast. This is the most critical part of flying any airplane, especially the B-47. This is the flying phase where everything has to be set up correctly prior to landing and any mistake could be catastrophic. It's busy enough with two pilots on board, with one reading a checklist and the other responding by flipping switches, setting flaps, lowering the landing gear, adjusting the power, trimming the aircraft and for night landings turning on the landing lights.

"Major Maxwell was now half-conscious and I convinced him to try to turn on the landing lights. He made eight or ten attempts before he finally turned them on. Coming into the GCA (Ground-Controlled Approach) pattern, they ran me into some moderate-to-severe turbulence and made it very difficult to fly the airplane. A couple of times I caught myself in 40 and 50-degree banks, with the airplane practically out of control.'

"Coming around the GCA pattern, I had no idea what my airspeed was but I was flying a constant 88 percent power setting. I could not see my airspeed indicator but I think it was a little bit slow because I encountered slight buffeting and stalls so I moved it up to about 94 percent. Then GCA lined me up on final but I couldn't hold any heading since I just couldn't make out the directional indicator."

Obie was on his own tonight and everything has to be from memory. No additional pilot on board to help read the checklist, to correct mistakes and to help out with the constant communication with ground control.

Barely able to see any of his instruments with the wind ripping at his eyes, he's flying mostly by feel. Feel the shudder – push the power up or lower the nose. Am I climbing or diving? What is my altimeter doing? Is it steady? Is the large needle going up or down? How can I trim the aircraft if I don't even know if I'm straight and level?

OK, time to put the gear down. Good, a solid clunk. Good indications, both gear down. Now push the power up. Retrim the aircraft.

"BINBROCK one six, your overshooting center line slightly. Turn left now to three, three zero, advise you're six and a half miles out. Stand by for your rate of descent." [3]

"Roger."

OK, flaps going down. Nose will go up so keep the nose down while I adjust the power and retrim. Right eye is hurting like the dickens! I'll keep it shut for a while.

"You're six miles out, farther to the right to three four zero, the runway heading, three four zero. You're dropping low, dropping low, level off. Three four zero, heading. You're overshooting way over to the left, right to three, five zero again, three five zero, coming back up to the glide path."

Obie has his power reduced for descent but he is unable to see his airspeed indicator. Again, he is flying by feel. He's adjusting his power based on what GCA is telling him about his position in relation to the glide path. Too high, reduce power slightly. Going below glide path bring the power back up. Up and down – adjust – keep wings level.

"Take her real easy Obie." [This is Major Doyle Reynolds, the Wing Training Officer. He'll be talking to Obie from the Control Tower.]

"GCA advised me I was too far to the left. I knew I just couldn't go around because I couldn't see much anymore and I couldn't see the airspeed indicator. I was flying final approach by just feel, so I made up my mind the only thing to do was to go on in.'

"BINBROCK one six. You're considerably left now at five miles, you're right on our glide path, right to due North, zero degrees. You're left of on course. Due North to heading, coming back into the center line, four and one half miles out about twenty feet below our glide path, coming up. You're now on our glide path heading back into your own course, real nice. On the glide path four miles from touch down."

"One Six, you're three and a half out. You're still pretty far left, left of on course. BINBROCK one six, Dyess GCA, advise. You're lined up too far left. Suggest you take it around if possible, advise please."

"I realized I would never be able to see the runway with my seat bottomed out, so I raised the seat to the full up position. I then looked over the side of the aircraft and surprisingly, in that clear air stream, I could see quite well. I must have gotten out of the path of all that dirt and debris that was blowing in my face.'

"This is one six, let's see here, what she looks like.'

"I saw the runway off to the right and made an immediate turn and then a roll out.'

"You'll have to turn her a little to the left, Obie, to get over to the right there and then swing her back."

"BINBROCK one six, coming in zero degree heading, now left to three four five, three four five turning into the runway."

"I 've got the runway in pretty good sights, am I high. low, or what?"

"Roger, you're about sixty feet above the glide path. You can ease it down just a little."

"Obie, you are a little bit too far to the right of the runway right now, unless you can line up on it. Do you look okay?"

"I feel pretty good up here."

"Okay, if you've got her, bring her in easy."

"One six, you're still up pretty high now, about eighty to ninety feet above the glide path, right on course."

"Take her easy, Obie, you've got her made."

"One six, you're right on course, one mile out, approximately ninety to a hundred feet high. Your coming down nicely."

"One six, you're now approximately fifty feet high, approaching end of runway."

"Just keep on coming down, Obie, you're a little high yet, bring her on down."

"Okay, start flying her real easy."

"Fly it real easy."

"Start easing your power off of her."

"As soon as you get a touch there, why ease that brake chute out."

"If she bounces there go ahead and pull your brake chute right now and drop your power."

"The round-out was ... I just stepped it down until I hit the ground and I immediately pulled the brake chute. After that, everything seemed normal. I landed about 4,500 feet down the runway."

148

"Put on your brakes, Obie, real easy now, easy on your brakes, you've got it made, buddy."

"You've got plenty of room. just hold your brakes real easy. Get her lined up down the center line, looking good, buddy, Just hold her right straight down the middle. Just ease your brakes on when you get her there and stop her and drop your power."

"I chopped No. 1, 2 and 5 immediately after touchdown and started knocking off everything as far as electrical goes."

"I'm going to leave the plane sit right out here. I'm afraid of this brute."

"Yeh, you just stop her there and just ease out of that seat."

"Roger."

"Real nice job, buddy, just slow her down and chop that power."

"Immediately upon stopping, I cut the other engines and was very cautious about getting out of my seat because I was almost sure it was going to trigger."

"I pulled the helmet bag that had been jamming the entrance hatch, opened the entrance door and exit from the aircraft now looked okay. As I climbed down the ladder a Fireman grabbed me. I yelled at him 'There's another man up there.' I would say I was on the ground about 20 seconds when I went completely blind due to the wind blast."

Obie and Major Maxwell were taken by ambulance to the hospital and sedated so they could rest overnight. The doctor found blood clots in Obie's eyes, with the right eye being the worst for wear.

While in the hospital, Major Maxwell told me that I could have used better terminology when I yelled at him "We're going in." He thought that meant we were going to crash. I don't remember saying that, but he swears by it.

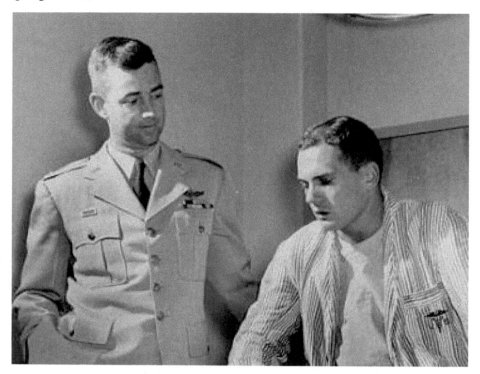

Major Maxwell visiting Obie in the Hospital

The Aircraft after flight.

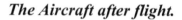

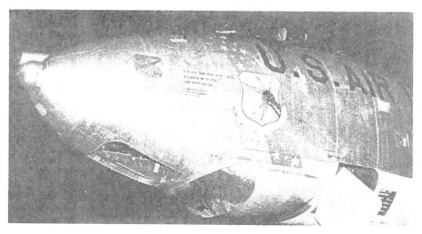

Navigators ejection escape hatch, just in front of the radome.

B-47 cockpit with the canopy missing.

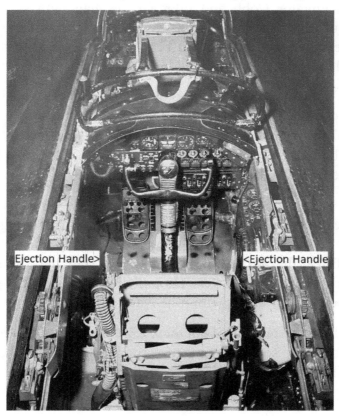

Both ejection handles had been raised and triggers pulled.

The author asked Obie what caused the seat ejection sequence to malfunction. He said, "The ejection seat malfunction was due to a broken pin. This was the pin that was supposed to fire and set off the explosive charge for the ejection.'

He also recalled how difficult it was to unstow the control column so he was able to fly the airplane. It took all of his strength to pull it out of the locked position. A maintenance technician later showed him the spring that was supposed to hold the column in the locked position and how it had been broken into 3 pieces.

The bailouts.

The navigator Cobb and pilot Graves had both successfully bailed out through the Nav's ejection hatch. Although both parachutes opened it was not the best of conditions. It was a black night and temperatures were well below zero.

Cobb's survival seat pack had come loose and was whacking him on the back as he fell toward the earth in free fall. It took him awhile to unhook it. A person can free fall from 34,000 feet in about 3 minutes before hitting the ground. As he fell through a bank of clouds, he finally pulled his rip cord. The chute opened with seconds to spare.

Graves who was hypoxic by now and afraid of passing out did just the opposite, he opened his chute immediately after he left the aircraft. But at this altitude along with being extremely cold, the air was almost devoid of oxygen. He pulled the cord on his portable oxygen bottle but was not sure if he was getting oxygen from it.

Both hit the ground hard but there were no serious injuries. They each made their separate way to farm houses in the vicinity of Dalhart, Texas and state police drove them back to Dyess.

An artist's depiction of the incident. [16]

MAN AGAINST ODDS

"SAKE" SHUFFERT '58

A 341st BW B-47, ON A NIGHT SSG MISSION, WAS CRUISING AT ALTITUDE NW OF AMARILLO. SUDDENLY A VIOLENT EXPLOSION ROCKED THE AIRCRAFT AND FIRE LIT UP THE RIGHT WING.

THE AC, CONVINCED THE WING WOULD GO AT ANY MINUTE, ORDERED HIS CREW TO BAIL OUT. THE NAVIGATOR EJECTED.

THE AC AND CP WENT THROUGH THE EJECTION CYCLE. THE CANOPY BLEW *BUT NEITHER SEAT WOULD FIRE !!!* THE COCKPIT WAS A ROARING MASS OF CONFUSION, WITH WIND BLAST THROUGH THE LOWER HATCH AND CANOPY OPENING. THE AC CLIMBED DOWN FROM HIS SEAT AND MADE HIS WAY OUT THE NAV. HATCH.

AS THE CP ALSO STRUGGLED TOWARD THE LOWER HATCH, HIS FOOT STRUCK SOMETHING. *IT WAS THE SSG INST NAVIGATOR --- OUT COLD!!!*

THE CP THOUGHT FAST. HE KNEW HE COULD NEVER GET THE SSG NAV OUT BEFORE HE TOO BECAME HYPOXIC. HE CLIMBED BACK INTO HIS SEAT. AS HE HOOKED UP HE LOOKED AT THE FIRE. No. 6 ENGINE WAS STREAMING FLAME. THE WING LOOKED INTACT, SO HE DIVED THE AIRCRAFT AND SHUT DOWN No. 6.

"ROGER 16, THIS IS ALTUS TOWER— WE UNDERSTAND—"

"16, THIS IS FATCHANCE— TAKE UP A HEADING OF 145 DEGREES—"

THE CP LEVELED OFF AT 13,500'. THE FIRE SUB-SIDED. NOW FLYING FROM THE BACK SEAT, HE WAS BEING WHIPPED BY THE SLIPSTREAM. HE SAT IN A SEAT THAT MIGHT FIRE AT ANY MOMENT. THE SSG NAV WAS CONCIOUS NOW BUT TOO GROGGY TO GET HIS CHUTE PACK ON. HE KEPT TRYING.

"YES, GEN POWER, WE HAVE HIM IN THE PATTERN NOW. HE'S DOING A GREAT JOB."

THE CP RADIOED HIS PREDICAMENT TO ALTUS TOWER AND GCI SITES. THEY GAVE HIM A STEER TO DYESS. HE WANTED TO TAKE IT HOME. DYESS WEATHER WAS 1500' OVERCAST. GCA SOON HAD HIM IN CONTACT AND BROUGHT HIM AROUND THE PATTERN FOR AN APPROACH. THE LONG FLIGHT WAS NEARING IT'S CLIMAX.

NOW THE PROBLEM OF LANDING LIGHTS AROSE. THE CP INSTRUCTED THE I.N. AND HE REACHED AROUND THE AC'S SEAT AND TURNED ON THE LIGHTS. LANDING THE B-47 FROM THE BACK SEAT, WITHOUT A CANOPY, AT NIGHT, AND ON 5 ENGINES WAS A FULL ISSUE OF PROBLEMS BUT LT. JAMES E. OBENAUF PUT THE MACHINE DOWN WITH PROFESSIONAL SKILL.

For his outstanding response to an aircraft emergency, Lieutenant Obenauf has been presented the DFC and becomes the first CP to receive the SAC Heads Up Flying Club award.

Chapter Six

Interview with the Wing Commander

We learn more about what happened during the flight based on this subsequent interview between Obie and Colonel Anthony Perna, the Wing Commander. This is the actual transcript.

Obenauf: As soon as the canopy went, I couldn't see anything.

Perna: Was your seat low enough? Do you think it came near hitting you?

Obenauf: No, I remember that canopy going right straight up in the air as far as I could see.

Perna: Did your cockpit lights stay on?

Obenauf: As best I could tell, they were all on.

Perna: Your visor was up and your mask was on or off?

Obenauf: My visor was up and my mask was on. I had full intentions of using my ejection. sequence. I squeezed it and that didn't work, and I thought maybe I hadn't pulled the handle hard enough and I yanked real hard and pulled the handles, tried the left one hard and tried the right, one hard, and tried to squeeze the trigger again.

Perna; Had your column stowed?

Obenauf: Yes, sir, By this time I made up my mind that I had to get out of there, for the flames were getting up the fuselage.

Perna: You released the (pressure) door, and did it slide down?

Obenauf: No, sir. It jammed ... a helmet bag was jammed in the door. I must have had hypoxia because it wouldn't have taken much imagination to figure out why that door was jammed. I didn't try at all to unjam it.

Perna: Were you on oxygen or off?

Obenauf: I was on normal oxygen. I didn't put it on emergency. I thought I would try to go to the observer's [navigator's]hatch and jump out. I assumed Major Graves ejected. That is when I saw Maxwell.

Perna: Were the lights on in the crawlway then?

Obenauf: Right, sir. I couldn't have seen without lights- I was half-blinded from dust.

Perna: Did you have your gloves on?

Obenauf: That is something I did immediately after I climbed back into the seat. My hands were getting cold. I think I had one glove on. I always keep my right glove off so I can write, I remember I was thinking, I've got to get this glove on. I had it right in my pocket.

Perna: When you got back in the seat you had to unlock the column?

Obenauf: Yes, sir. I tried to engage the column once and I had trouble, and I tried again and I got it the second time..., I remember I engaged it and the wheel was cocked real funny and I disengaged it and did it again.

Perna: The airplane was still on autopilot?

Obenauf: Yes, sir.

Perna: And, it was still burning at this time?

Obenauf: At this time I realized that the fire wasn't half as bad as we had originally thought. It was just on the outer section of the wing. I didn't know it was just the engine; I just knew it was outboard.

Perna: Did you stopcock the engine then or later?

Obenauf: I don't think I stopcocked it then, sir; I didn't realize it was an engine fire. I couldn't see the engine itself.

Perna: Were you able to hold your head against the slipstream or was the windshield breaking it all for you?

Obenauf: By maintaining close to 200 knots, the stream was much less.

Perna: Did you knock it off autopilot right then?

Obenauf: I was still on autopilot till I looked the situation over. I must have been hypoxic; there was a period in there before I got the oxygen on emergency. It seemed like a matter of minutes before I started descent.

Perna: When did you stopcock the engine?

Obenauf: It was some time during my descent. I said to myself, "I've just gotta start thinking," I had an awful time forcing myself to think. The engine burned itself out in about five minutes."

Perna: Did you fasten the safety belt when you got back in the seat?

Obenauf: No, sir. I couldn't fasten it; I had an awful time trying to find anything. I just couldn't think.   I had an awful time trying to maintain control.

Perna: Did you put the gear down?

Obenauf: No, sir I was going to put it down but, in my mind, I kept thinking that I couldn't bail out with my gear down. I think it would have been better if I had let it down.

Perna: How much speed did you pick up?

Obenauf: I think it was about 280 to 300.

Perna: At what speed were you when you started this decent?

Obenauf: About 230 knots, sir. Major Graves had it set in Idle, because when I climbed up in the cockpit the first thing I did was try to pull the power back but it was already at idle.

Perna: Did you land with your safety belt undone?

Obenauf: Yes, sir.

Perna: What altitude did you level out at?

Obenauf: I remember one time at 11,000, That is where I lost my oxygen, I was on 100 percent emergency and I couldn't breathe; I had to go back to normal oxygen in order to keep breathing. I didn't dare to take the mask off for that was really protecting my face.

Perna: Was there any debris in the air or any weight besides the dirt?

Obenauf: I saw something, that flew up and went over me. I thought it was a sextant. Our clipboard also came through there.

Perna: Did you ever get Major Maxwell on the interphone?

Obenauf: Yes, sir. I told him to hit me on the leg to acknowledge anything I said to him.

Perna: You switched to guard on your UHF control box?

Obenauf: Yes, sir. I switched before I ever called. I thought I was transmitting maydays but I wasn't even connected. That is another thing that indicates I must have been half-hypoxic.

Perna: Could you see the airspeed indicator?

Obenauf: I could tell where the needle was; I could tell within 15 or 20 knots

Perna: Did you ever get pitched up off the seat when you hit rough air?

Obenauf: No, sir, I never once hit any trouble. I was being held down more than pushed up; in fact, I was getting pushed hard backward.

Chapter Seven

Obie's Awards

For his heroism, Lt. Obenauf received the Distinguished Flying Cross, the Cheney Award, the Aviator's Valor Award, and the Koren Kolligian trophy.

The Distinguished Flying Cross:

This medal is awarded for extraordinary achievement while participating in aerial flight. Both heroism and achievement must be entirely distinctive, involving operations that are not routine. Obie joins a distinguished society of other recipients of this award which was first presented to Capt. Charles A. Lindbergh, of the U.S. Army Corps Reserve, for his solo flight of 3,600 miles across the Atlantic in 1927.

General Thomas Power, the Commander in Chief of the Strategic Air Command had been listening in on the Dyess conversations with Obie as he brought the B-47 down for a successful landing.

He was so impressed with what Obie had done that he called the Pentagon from his headquarters in Nebraska and talked to General Curtis LeMay the Vice Chief of Staff of the Air Force. He wanted to award the Distinguished Flying Cross to Obie. LeMay agreed, and within 36 hours after Obie had touched down General Power flew to Dyess, went to the base theater and in front of a standing room only crowd pinned the medal on Obie.

It was a complete surprise to Obie as he had been brought from the base hospital where he was still under medical care.

Obie receiving the Distinguished Flying Cross from General Power.

The Kolligian Trophy:

This trophy was established in 1958 and recognizes outstanding airmanship by an aircrew member. The award's namesake, 1st Lt. Koren Kolligian Jr., was declared missing in the line of duty when his T-33 Shooting Star disappeared off the coast of California in 1955.

The crew member must show extraordinary skill, alertness, ingenuity and/or proficiency in averting or minimizing the seriousness of a flight mishap.

The Kolligian trophy being presented to Obie. Pat is by his side, Kolligian family on the right. In General Curtis LeMay's office in the Pentagon, 7 May 1959

Obie and General LeMay holding the Kolligian Trophy.

Here is Obie receiving the Koren Kolligian trophy in General Lemay's office in the Pentagon, when Lemay was Vice Chief of Staff. The following citation was read at the award ceremony.

Koren Kolligian trophy, Summary of Achievement.

"First Lieutenant James E. Obenauf, B-47 copilot of the 341st Bombardment Wing, Dyess Air Force Base, Texas, displayed conspicuous skill and fortitude 28 April 1958 to save his unconscious navigator and to bring his damaged bomber back safely after an in-flight fire and subsequent bailout of the other two crew members.'

"While on a night navigation and bombing training mission the B-47 on which Lieutenant Obenauf was co-pilot experienced oil pressure difficulty with number 3 engine. A short time later while cruising at 34,000 feet the aircraft was rocked by an explosion. The aircraft commander looked toward number three engine and observed the reflection of a fire which he assumed to be in the fuselage. He ordered the crew to abandon the aircraft.'

"The ejection seat of both the aircraft commander and the co-pilot failed to fire. The aircraft commander and the navigator had left the aircraft through the navigator's lower escape hatch and were being followed by Lieutenant Obenauf when he saw the instructor navigator lying unconscious in the aisle.'

"Confronted with the unenviable choice of saving himself by bailing out or facing what appeared to be certain death by staying with the aircraft in an attempt to save his fellow officer, Lieutenant Obenauf returned immediately to his seat. The ejection seat was armed and might fire at any moment. The aircraft was burning violently and in danger of exploding. The canopy and the downward escape hatch were gone, filling the cockpit with frigid air. In addition he had the problem of making a successful night landing alone.'

"Lieutenant Obenauf promptly put the B-47 into a steep descent in order that his companion might have a chance to regain consciousness in the lower altitude. At 11,000 feet the instructor navigator became semiconscious and Lieutenant Obenauf succeeded in extinguishing the blaze.'

"Despite temperatures as low as minus 30 degrees Centigrade, in which his hands became so cold he could scarcely control the aircraft, and wind blast, cockpit debris, and cold that blinded him until he couldn't read his instruments clearly, Lieutenant Obenauf continued to struggle with the aircraft. He was able to make radio contact with another aircraft in the vicinity which relayed instructions from a DF station. Ultimately establishing communications with a GCI station, he maneuvered the plane into a local GCA pattern and followed instructions to a successful landing at his home base.'

"His heroism, valor and professional airmanship were superlative. His courage, conduct and professional skill under extremely adverse conditions were in the highest tradition of the United States Air Force."

The Koren Kolligian trophy has been awarded continuously for the past 62 years. It was first awarded in 1957. Obie was the second recipient of the award in 1958. The third recipient in 1959 was First Lieutenant Ronald L. Warner who happened to be the author's roommate at Malden Air Base Missouri. We were both Aviation Cadets undergoing pilot training, before I transferred to navigation training.

It is interesting to note that only 5 of the 62 awards have been given to First Lieutenants. Most were given to Captains, Majors, and Lt. Colonels.

The Cheney Award:

This is an aviation award presented in memory of 1st Lt. William H. Cheney, who was killed in an air collision over Italy in 1918. It was established in 1927, and is awarded to an airman for an act of valor, extreme fortitude or self-sacrifice in a humanitarian interest, performed in connection with an aircraft. The award includes an inscribed bronze plaque and honorarium of $500.

It was presented to Obie on July 14th 1959 in the Pentagon by General Curtis LeMay,

165

The Cheney Award, 14 July 1959

Handshake after the Cheney award. Pat proudly looking on.

Heads up Flying Award, presented by Major General Archie Olds.

The Aviator's Valor Award:

Shortly after the end of World War II, an annual Valor Award presentation was initiated by the American Legion Aviators' Post No. 743 to recognize a military aviator who performed a feat of valor during the prior year as determined by an Aviators' Post panel.

The Valor Award was written into official Air Force regulations in 1953. In 1970, it was expanded to include a member of each of the three services who performed "a conspicuous act of valor or courage during an aerial flight" the preceding year. Valor Award recipients are now chosen at the highest levels of their respective service and

167

approved by the office of the corresponding Chief of Staff. Aviators' Post Valor Award recipients are a select few and represent a proud tradition. The first recipient of the award was General Henry "Hap" Arnold, Commander of the Army Air Forces during World War II.

Meeting with Senators

Senator Everick Dirkson, Illinois

Senator, Paul Douglas, Illinois

Chapter Eight

Above All the Other Awards

For all the awards Obie received, this is what he cherishes the most. It's what the Instructor Navigator, Major Joe Maxwell remembers on how Obie saved his life.

My Second Chance to Live

"Here's what a brush with death six miles up taught this flyer. We were over the Texas Panhandle at 34,000 feet. Just before 11 p.m. April 28 No. 6 engine of our Strategic Air Command jet bomber exploded and engulfed the right wing in flames. The order was given, 'Bail Out!'

"The pilots blew off the canopy to clear their ejection track upward into the night.'

"That's all I remember of this phase of the ordeal. The canopy de-compression blast tore my helmet loose, slammed me against a bulkhead and knocked me unconscious. I lay in the darkness, my chute pack gone, my oxygen mask ripped from my face, my life draining away.'

"What followed appears miraculous: the ejection seat of Lt. James E. Obenauf failed to fire. He tried to bail out of the entrance

hatch, but it jammed. As he started forward to the navigator's ejection hatch, he stumbled over me in the dark passageway.'

"The plane was on fire and seemed about to break up. But Lieutenant Obenauf did not jump. He climbed back into his dangerously hot ejection seat and with all the skill and prayer he could muster flew the seemingly doomed 90-ton, six-engine jet single-handed. During his rapid descent to save me, and all the way home, a terrific wind tore at his face unmercifully. Almost an hour later, when he arrived over Dyess Air Force Base, he was nearly blind. And yet, descending through heavy clouds and turbulence, he managed an 'impossible, one-man landing. The man who might have simply jumped and saved himself had brought me back from the dead.'

"Next morning, the sun poured down with a special warmth. I had a fresh viewpoint on everything around me. I realized I had been given what many people wish for: a second chance at life. The pressure and problems of everyday life seem easy for me now.'

"To Jim Obenauf I'll be forever grateful. His courageous action makes it possible for me to guide my six children through their important formative years. I feel that his decision was primarily a reflection of the way he grew up, the character of his way of life. And that will remain always an inspiration for me and my children.'[5]

Obie flew in the B-47 from 1956 to 1962 while at Dyess AFB, Texas with close to 3,000 hours accrued as both copilot and pilot. Six months after this incident he was upgraded from copilot to pilot, becoming one of the youngest Aircraft Commanders in all of Strategic Air Command.

Chapter Nine

The TV Star

To Tell the Truth

"To Tell the Truth" was a television game show where four celebrity panelists were presented with three contestants. The panelists must identify which one was the actual person whose unusual experience had been read out by the show's moderator. When the panelists questioned the contestants, two of them may lie but the actual person must tell the truth.

Obie appeared on the show that aired March 10th 1959. The moderator was Bud Collyer and the panelists were Ralph Bellamy, Kitty Carlisle, Tom Poston and Betty White. Obie appears in his flying suit along with two men pretending to be Obie.

When it came time to identify the real James Edward Obenauf, Major Joe Maxwell came on stage to identify Obie.

Here's the young 37 year old Betty White on that show. Today [2020] Betty is 98 years old.

This is Your Life

This Is Your Life was an NBC television show where the host would surprise guests and then take them through a retrospective of their life in front of an audience. Ralph Edwards hosted the show.

Here's Obie being greeted by his navigator, Lieutenant John Cobb.

Major Joe Maxwell, Wing Commander Perna and pilot' Major James Graves [on the right]

Obie's father brought Obie's two sons to the show.

Chapter Ten
Obie the B-58 Driver

In 1962 Obie was selected by his wing commander to transition to the B-58, a Mach-2 bomber.

Because the B-58 was so technologically advanced, the Strategic Air Command wanted only the very best pilots and navigators to fly it. You could not volunteer for the B-58 program, you had to be selected by your wing commander.

175

The B-58 Hustler was a four engine, delta wing bomber, capable of speeds in excess of Mach 2 (twice the speed of sound). At its maximum speed of Mach 2.2 (1,452 mph) it was 2½ times faster than the muzzle velocity of a .45 caliber bullet. Although it was a strategic bomber it could out maneuver, out turn, and out climb most fighter aircraft of its day.

Whereas the B-47 carried a crew of three: two pilots and one navigator, the B-58 carried one pilot and two navigators. One of the two navigators was a navigator/bombardier and the other was a defensive systems operator. Each crew member sat in their own escape capsule, as shown here.

The B-58 began its operational career in 1960 and it was years ahead of its time in technological innovation. People soon started taking notice of this 'new guy' on the block. Windows began rattling as B-58s began breaking the sound barrier on training flights.

Before it was fully combat ready, a B-58 crew, competing against more experienced B-47 and B-52 bomber crews, did the unthinkable. It took first place for bombing accuracy at the 1960, Strategic Air Command, Bombing Competition.

This bomber went on to capture numerous international speed records winning five aeronautical trophies. It also set 14 world speed records in international competition.

The wing commander at Dyess Air Force Base had no problem selecting one of his best B-47 pilots to enter the B-58 program. Obie was at the top of his list for being the best of the best. Obie flew B-58s at Grissom Air Force Base from 1962 to 1970. That's where the author met Obie. I was at Grissom from 1966 to 1969 as a navigator/bombardier in the B-58.

Fred Vatcher DSO, Leon Wilson Nav, James "Obie" Obenauf, Pilot.

December 1964, Capt. James "Obie" Obenauf, Pilot; Capt. A.D. Soderberg, Navigator; Capt. F.M. Vatcher, DSO; Obie shakes hands with his Crew Chief and Asst. Crew Chief.

George MacDonald also flew B-58s. George MacDonald and the author are current members of the B-58 Association's Board of Directors.

Chapter Eleven

Obie in Retirement

James Obenauf retired from the Air Force in 1974 with the rank of Lt. Colonel. Among his career assignments were Dyess AFB, TX from 1956 to 1962 (B-47s). Grissom AFB, IN, where he flew in the B-58 from 1962 to 1970. Commander, 9th SOS DaNang, AB, Viet Nam in 1970. Commander, 100th OMS, Davis-Monthan, AFB, AZ from 1971 to 1972. Director, Recon Maintenance, 15th AF, CA from 1972 to 1974.

After retirement from the Air Force, Jim returned to his hobby of manufacturing furniture and cabinets from 1974 to 1994. He has been involved in consulting for furniture building and design from 1994 until the present.

Obie and Pat had four children. Dave who was born in 1957, Dan in 1958, Nancy in 1961, and Susan in 1963. When Obie retired from the Air Force in 1974, the family moved to Tucson, Arizona. Pat died in 1998 from cancer. He is now married to the former Linda Shand.

Obie continued with his love of flying after leaving the Air Force. For 27 years from 1977 – 2004 he flew gliders and also the tow planes that took those gliders into the air. He had a total of 400 hours in gliders and 410 hours in tow planes.

Obie towing a glider.

During this time he also owned a 1961 Piper Comanche for 17 years and had many good trips in this aircraft.

Piper Comanche

Obie's children: left to right: Susan, Dan, David, and Nancy

Linda and Obie Obenauf

As Obie said in his latest correspondence, "I've been lucky twice in my life, 2 great ladies."

The End

George Holt, Jr.

RESEARCH NOTES

1. The author had numerous phone conversations and Email correspondence with Obie from 17 Feb 2020 to 25 April 2020. He answered questions about his family life – children, marriage to Pat, more details about the explosion event, and the events after the explosion, etc. He did not get to actually use the sextant on that mission.

2. "The Dawn of Discipline" by Walter J. Boyne, AIR & SPACE MAGAZINE, JULY 2009

3. TRANSCRIPT FROM TAPE RECORDING OF RADIO COMMUNICATICNS RECEIVED AND TRANSMITTED AT DYESS AIR FORCE BASE,TEXAS, 28 APRIL 1958. PERTAINING TO AN AIRCRAFT INCIDENT (B -47)

4. "THE DECISION OF A LIFETIME," Jim Obenauf's Story. The Strategic Air Command Combat Crew Magazine, issue of August, 1958.

5. "My Second Chance To Live" an article written by Major Joseph Maxwell and featured in the Dallas Morning News.

6. From the Boeing history page
https://www.boeing.com/history/products/b-47-stratojet.page

7. Federation of American Scientists https://fas.org/nuke/guide/usa/bomber/b-47.htm

8. "Twenty Seconds to Live" by Elizabeth Land. Copyright 1959 by Elizabeth Land and James Obenauf. A book containing information on the personal lives of the crew.

9. "THE DECISION OF A LIFETIME" COMBAT CREW: MAGAZINE OF THE STRATEGIC AIR COMMAND, VOLUMES IX NO 2 AUGUST 1958

10 Congressional Record page 7199, To be First Lieutenants in the Regular Air Force, James E. Obenauf AO3057997 https://www.govinfo.gov/content/pkg/GPO-CRECB-1959-pt6/pdf/GPO-CRECB-1959-pt6-1-2.pdf

11. The Development of Strategic Air Command, 1946-1981: A Chronological History, BY J. C. HOPKINS, SHELDON A. GOLDBERG, UNITED SATTES. AIR FORCE. STRATEGIC AIR COMMAND. OFFICE OF THE HISTORIAN

12. Marshall Michel - Air & Space Magazine | 8 May 2003
http://www.airspacemag.com/military-aviation/cit-michel.html

13. Obie had excellent recall of all the events during and after the explosion and fire, but almost no recall of events before the incident. From takeoff to explosion it took 2 hours for them to pass Amarillo. Amarillo is only about 30 minutes from Dyess. Whether or not the crew performed a celestial nav mission, a bomb run, a refueling or anything else could not be determined. Obie mentioned he could hear the nav and the instructor nav chatting, so the author constructed this dialogue as a conversation that could have taken place during this time frame.

14. "The B-47's Deadly Dominance" by Walter J. Boyne, Air Force Magazine ,Jan. 30, 2013

15. "The Obenauf Story" a film directed by George Sherman, written by Fredric M. Frank, produced by James Fonda, executive producer William Sackheim

16. This artist's depiction of the incident appeared in the June 1958 issue of Combat Crew Magazine. Jake Shuffert was the artist.

17. Dyess history –
https://www.dyess.af.mil/Fact-sheets/Display/Article/812832/dyess-history/

ABOUT THE AUTHOR

George Holt Jr. is a retired Air Force Colonel. He flew in numerous aircraft including the supersonic B-58. He had a tour in the Pentagon, went to Air War College and was twice a Wing Commander – once at Davis Monthan AFB, Arizona as commander of a Titan II ICBM wing, and then Grand Forks, North Dakota as commander of a Minuteman II ICBM wing. He was a Director at the National Defense University and also Director of Operations (J3) for US Forces Japan (USFJ).

After retirement, he formed AdaRose Inc., an employee-owned firm producing software for military battlefield systems including the Paladin self-propelled howitzer.

He has authored a number of other books. All are available on Amazon.

Author, George "Sonny" Holt

The following pages contain the appendices to:

Heroes I've Known

Part 1.

George T. MacDonald

11 Year Old Prisoner of War.

APPENDIX A

Babies born in Los Baños Prison Camp[32]

Bowie, Lea Lourdes	F	American	7/16/1944
Browne, Leslie Colvin Jr.	M	American	1/2/1945
Bucher, George Scott	M	American	1/30/1942
Carlson, Lawrence Ray	M	American	2/24/1942
Casanave, Peter Albert	M	American	1/9/1945
Clingen, Elizabeth Ruth "Betty"	F	American	3/1/1945
Craven, Henry Truxton	M	American	12/18/1944
Fox, Christopher Charles	M	British	9/9/1943
Francisco, Elizabeth	F	American	2/14/1945
Haven, Lewis Quincy "Skip" III	M	American	5/28/1945
Hess, Victor Glenn	M	American	8/12/1942
Lacey, Kristin	F	American	10/27/1944
MacWilliam, Scott	M	British	4/16/1942
McCoy, Lois Kathleen	F	American	2/20/1945
Nash, Roy Leslie	M	American	5/24/1943
O'Hara, Kathleen Francis	F	American	6/24/1942
O'Hara, Michael Joseph Jr.	M	American	8/11/1944
Plowman, Claire Elizabeth	F	American	6/2/1942
Plowman, Patricia Elaine	F	American	1/28/1945
Russell, Diana Marie	F	American	3/27/1942
Scaff, Lawrence Alvin	M	American	4/22/1942
Scherer, Richard	M	American	11/1/1944
Scheuermann, Dennis Friday	M	American	3/5/1942
Sechrist, John William	M	American	2/22/1942
Sherk, Gerry Ann	M	American	1/23/1944
Thomas, Dollie Mae	F	American	11/22/1942
Thomas, Elizabeth Francisco	F	American	2/14/1945
Thomas, Florence Ada	F	American	12/16/1941
Tulloch, William James	M	American	11/11/1944
Vigano, Maria Victoria	F	Italian	12/2/1942
Wichman, Douglas Jonathan	M	American	9/12/1942
Wightman, William Dana	M	British	6/29/1944
Wilson, Anita Marie	F	American	11/16/1944

APPENDIX B

Marriages in Los Baños Prison Camp [32]

Louise Charmian Boomer and Charles Gordon Mock   Apr. 19, 1944

Luckey Kathlyn Charter (Canadian) and Jay Augustus Hinkley Apr. 1944

Charlotte Kingsbury Lee and Lewis Quincy "Red" Haven Jr.   1945

Mildred Ailene Palmer and Oscar Gervius "Mac" McCoy   Apr. 18, 1944

Joan Marie Smith (British) and Jesse Smith Wilson   about 1943

APPENDIX C

Roster of 11 Navy Nurses at Los Baños

The following Navy nurses were sent from Santo Tomas Civilian Internment Camp to the Internment Camp at Los Baños in May 1943. They were the only U.S. Active Military in the Camp.

Cobb, Laura M.	Chief Nurse
Chapman, Mary F.	LTJG
Evans, Bertha R.	LTJG
Gorzelanski, Helen C.	LTJG
Harrington, Mary R.	LTJG
Nash, Margaret A,	LTJG
O'Haver, Goldie A.	LTJG
Paige, Eldene E.	LTJG
Pitcher, Susie J.	LTJG
Still, Dorothy	LTJG
Todd, C. Edwina	LTJG

Lieutenant Junior Grade, or LTJG, is the second commissioned officer rank in the United States Navy, and is equivalent to the rank of First Lieutenant in other branches of the Armed Services.

APPENDIX D

LOS BAÑOS INTERNEES

American, Australian, British, Canadian, Dutch, Italian, Norwegian, and Polish internees are listed. The author compiled the list from various sources, among them;
- The 40th Anniversary Program, Los Baños Liberation, February 23rd, 1985, Hunters ROTC Association Inc. 1985.
- The Camp Census of February 1945.
- The Census Report of American Prisoners at Los Baños compiled on December 25th 1944, showing age, sex, and occupation for each American internee.
- Many errors have been corrected e.g., added the names of two babies born just days before the rescue and some misspelled names have been corrected. Females married in the camp have been listed under their maiden names as well as being placed together with their husbands.[33]

AMERICANS (with Age)

Adams, Elbridge M. 62
Adams, Gustav Adolph 29
Adams, Owen 66
Adams, Welba S. 59
Adrian, Kathleen Halloran 34
Adrian, Michael Joseph 40
Agnes, Sister Inelda 35
Agnes, Sister Regina 37
Ahern, Hilary 33
Aimee, Sister Marie 41
Aiton, Joe E. 50
Aiton, Felicimo L. 16
Aiton, Josepha D. 50
Albert, Daniel Louis 37
Ale, Francis Harvey 39
Allen, Robert Coleman 32
Alness, Mark Gerhard 61
Alphonsa, Sister Mary 53

Alsobrook, Anthony Leonidas 38
Amstutz, Elda 45
Ancilla, Sister Marie 27
Anderson, Charles Richard 39
Anderson, Charles Stewart 54
Anderson, Theodore Maxwell 33
Anderson, Oscar .William 60
Ankney, William Edgar 52
Antoinette, Sister M. 42
Andrew, Sister Mary 59
Apelseth, Clement Anders 53
Appleby, Blanche 57
Aquinata, Sister M. 37
Arana, Bernardina 51
Arana, Esther 24
Arana, Cesar 22
Arick, Melvin Ray 30
Arida, Jodat Kamel 41

Armstrong, Robert Worthington 59

Ashton, Sidney 28

Assumpta, Sister M. 50

Augustus, Sister Mary 58

Avery, Charles William 53

Avery, Henry 59

Axtman, Boniface 35

Ayres, Glen Edwin 46

Babbitt, Winfred Howard 72

Backman, Herbert 37

Bagby, Calvin T. 28

Baker, Rowland John 45

Balano, Felix 47

Baldwin, Rena 53

Barnaby, Catherine 43

Barnes, Charles Irwin 37

Barnes, Evelyn Crew 38

Barnes, Richard Porter 39

Barter, Fred 56

Bartgis, Fred 60

Barth, Phyllis Ludwig 43

Bartlett, Mildred Glaze 39

Bartlett, Sydney Stockholm 44

Barton, Roy Franklin 61

Bateman, Jack 15

Bateman, John James 20

Bateman, Sallie 13

Bauman, William McComb 19

Baxter, Cecil Marie 39

Baxter, Sidney 42

Bayley, Harold Raymond 33

Bayouth, Khallel Assad 61

Beaber, H. 37

Beata, Sister M. 43

Beaty, Truman Carlson 31

Bebell, Clifford Fel ix Swift 38

Beck, Emsley William 37

Beck, Francis Harold 37

Becker, Frank Emil 42

Bee, Edwin Joseph 24

Beeman, Frank Robert 18

Beeman, Maude Rona 26

Beeman, Narvel Chester 51

Beeman, Raymond Richard 20

Beeman, Wallace Earl 23

Begley, Charlie 52

Beigbeder, Frank Michael 46

Bennett, Frank Cantillo 47

Benninghoven, Edward Robert 42

Berger, William Harris 49

Bergman, Gerda Ottelia 57

Besser, Leo 38

Bezotte, Fred 56

Billings, Bliss W. 63

Binsted, Norman S. 54

Binsted, Willie M. G. 55

Birsh, Charles 46

Bissinger, George Henry 55

Bissinger, Winifred Allen 42

Bittner, Joseph 39

Blackledge, David 12

Blackledge, Helen 36

Blackledge, Robert 6

Blair, Herbert E. 65

Blair, Susan 68

Blake, Lila 42

Blake, Mary 67

Blake, Owen A. 39

Blakeley, Mildred M. 61

Blalock, John 32

Blanchard, Harold Mason 48

Blanton, Charles Maxwell 68

Blanton, Dale Lincoln 48

Blechynden, Claire Louise 25

Blue, Harry Coleman 31

Bogacz, Francis 30

Bogle, Edwin Carmel 46
Bolderston, Constance 42
Bollman, Benjamin B. 39
Bollman, Elsie K. 35
Bollman, J. W. 8
Bollman, Lynn B. 3
Bond, Leo 37
Bonham, Rex 30
Boomer, Louise Charmian 28
Boomer, Joseph 72
Boston, William 67
Boswell, Eleanor Madaline 21
Bousman, H. 50
Bousman, James 13
Bousman, Martha 9
Bousman, Nona 44
Bousman, Tom 15
Bowker, Bayard Jordan 62
Bowie, Harold Dewell 30
Bowie, Leah Lourdes 1
Bowie, Paquita Rodriguez 29
Boyce, Leila Susan 26
Boyce, Viola Ceres 21
Boyd, Joseph 46
Boyens, Ernest 60
Boyers, James Simon 28
Boyle, Philip 29
Bradfield, Elizabeth Shortridge 49
Bradley, Grant 69
Bradney, Reuel 43
Bradanauer, Frederick W. 40
Bradanauer, Grace A. 34
Bratton, Charles Henley 38
Brazee, Albert John Jr. 40
Brazee, Nancy Agnes Erwin 43
Brendel, Oswood Roland 29
Brigitine, Sister 43
Brink, John William 14

Brink, Maude E. 46
Brink, Myron 51
Brink, Pamela 10
Brink, Robert Arlington 13
Broad, Wilfred 31
Brock, Joe O. 54
Brockway, Alex Grove 44
Brockway, Merna Morris 34
Brook, Walter Leroy 54
Brooks, Horace 66
Brown, George 28
Brown, Harry John 64
Brown, Helen Margaret 37
Brown, Katherine Ellis 40
Brown, Mary Martha 26
Brown, Nell McAfee 65
Brown, Ray 65
Brown, Richard Sefton 59
Brown, Roy H. 67
Browne, Leslie 30
Browne, Pilar 26
Browne, Robert 61
Brush, John Burk 32
Brush, Lois Bogue 22
Brushfield, Elizabeth 38
Bryan, Arthur 68
Bryan, Edgar Robeson 37
Bryan, Winifred 45
Bucher, Anna L. 9
Bucher, George Scott 2
Bucher, Henry H. 36
Bucher, Henry H. Jr. 8
Bucher, Louise S. 35
Bucher, Priscilla J. 7
Buckalew, Donald Howland 21
Buckles, Frank Woodruff 43
Budlong, Vinton Alva 53
Burke, Harry Taylor 34

Burkman, Charles Harris 53
Burlingame, Walter Michael 50
Burnham, Edward Frank 23
Burns, Francis 40
Burns, James 45
Burns, James 62
Burrell, Louie Grant 35
Burton, Edith Canz 30
Burton, Harry Royal 68
Burton, James Edward 39
Butler, John Nicholsen 42
Butler, Linnie Marie 44
Cadwallader, Helen 35
Caecilius, Sister M. 25
Cain, Claude Oliver 46
Cain, Thomas 33
Caldwell, William A. 66
Calhoun, Alexander Dewey 46
Callaway, Cleve 59
Calvert, John Ellis 45
Calve, Elisa Warbaugh 24
Cammack, Larue 47
Campbell, Guilford E. 77
Campbell, Leo Lee 52
Campp, Antony L. 52
Canson, John 65
Capen, Morris Noel 21
Caritas, Sister M. 53
Carlisle, Mabel Burris 48
Carlson, Alvin 39
Carlson, Imogene Ina 32
Carlson, Lawrence 1
Carlson, Mark 3
Carlucci, John (Boniface) 48
Carpenter, Henry 36
Carson, Hilton 67
Carter, John H. 71
Carter, Roland van 52

Carty, George B. 38
Carty, Eleanor May 29
Carty, Jean Pearl 7
Casanave, Andres 36
Casanave, Emilio 38
Casanave, Grete 22
Casanave, Pedro Jr. 33
Casanave, Pedro Andres 76
Casanave, Peter A. 9
Casanave, Rachel Olive 42
Casanave, Teresa E. 56
Casanave, Theodore 47
Casey, Edward 65
Cashman, Michael 27
Cassel, Henry D. 55
Cassell, Marie 48
Cassell, Marion Reedy 21
Cassell, Maurice Arnold 23
Cassidy, John Patrick 33
Catherine, Sister M. 49
Cease, Forrest Lee 69
Cecil, Robert E. 38
Celeste, Sister M. 49
Chambers, Bunnie Sr. 37
Chambers, Bunnie Jr. 4
Chambers, Isidra 29
Chambers, Katherine 4
Chambers, Maria 8
Chantal, Sister M. de 42
Chapman, Corwin Clyde 57
Chapman, Mary Frances 30
Chapman, Virginia Dewey 36
Chase, Leland Preston 28
Chatman, Littleton 61
Cheek, Jesse Willard 29
Chester, Harold Dean 33
Chester, Pearl Eileen 26
Chestnut, James Edward 44

Chew, John Hamilton 53
Chichester, Robert Oxley 27
Chickese, Ernest 25
Childers, Ralph Leroy 29
Christensen, Edward 68
Christensen, Joseph 53
Christie, A. 34
Chisholm, Robert 30
Cillo, Thomas 14
Clare, Joseph-Mother M. 42
Clark, Andrew 64
Clark, Rush Spencer 27
Claude, Henry Louie 53
Clayton, Noel 64
Clifford, Carl Gaines 69
Clifford, William Dennis 57
Clingen, Herbert Signer 29
Clingen, Ida Ruth 28
Clingen, Robert Fraser 2
Cobb, Laura May 48
Coffey, Henry A. 68
Cochran, Donald Lewellyn 52
Cofer, Newton 68
Coggeshall, Roland Roberts 38
Cogswell, Gladys Jessie 48
Cole, Birnie 60
Cole, George Edward 29
Cole, Minnie 29
Coleman, Barbara M. 19
Coleman, Marjorie K. 42
Coleman, Marshall L. 49
Coleman, Patricia C. 13
Colin, Paul J. 65
Collier, Leonard Hooper 26
Collins, Joseph Davis 40
Collins, Thomas James 47
Colman, Sister 42
Conant, Ellsworth Thomas 66

Conant, Juanda June 26
Conant, Myra Belle 55
Cone, Hector Anthony 42
Congleton, Lucy E. 37
Conner, Herman Burt 62
Connors, John 33
Conway, Joseph Michael 53
Constance, Sister M. 40
Cook, James William 42
Cook, Maude Rose 64
Cook, William Sherman 70
Cook, W. Thomas 63
Cooper, Alfred D. 58
Cooper, Hugh Price 54
Copello, Thomas George 53
Copper, Robert Gamble 29
Corbett, Daniel 28
Cornelison, Bernice 53
Cort, Marcus Robert 54
Corwin, Alvah Oatis 52
Crabb, Josephine Rosalie 32
Craven, Louise Broad 28
Craven, Osgood Coit 30
Crawford, Joseph Claypole 32
Crawford, Robert Allan 39
Crawford, Virginia Hale 31
Crist, Ann Bennett 42
Crist, Lynn Levi 50
Croft, Selma Marion 50
Croft, Patty Gene 19
Croft, William Frederick 17
Croisant, Everett Albert 34
Cromwell, Robert Horace 50
Croney, Dorothy Fain 33
Crooks, William 69
Crosby, George Howard 33
Crothers, Ellen N. 61
Crothers, John Young 63

Cullens, James Wimberly 49
Cullum, Leo 43
Cumming, Clarence Warder 54
Cumming, Patrick 46
Cummings, Ernest 51
Cummings, Milton Weston 73
Cunningham, Frederick Noel 34
Curavo, Leonard Alexander 40
Curran, Elmer Hege 56
Curran, Howard H. 29
Curran, Hugh McCollum Sr. 69
Curran, Hugh McCollum Jr. 30
Custer, Theodore Hart 39
Dahlke, Gustav A. 32
Dahlke, Inga Hedwig 32
Dakin, Bess May 42
Dakin, Charles Austin 52
Dale, Billie Ann 6
Dale, Donna Lee 7
Dale, Edna Lee 29
Dale, Frank Emmit 57
Dale, Melvin Eugene 33
Dale, Roberta M. 4
Damrosch, Elizabeth H. 29
Damrosch, Leopold 31
Damrosch, Leopold Jr. 2
Danie, Amelia Louise 57
Danie, Antony Joseph 49
Davey, Laura Emily 58
David, Sister M. 39
Davidson, Abraham 40
Davidson, Arthur Dewain 46
Davis, Marian Electra 36
Davis, Maureen Neal 30
Davis, Roger William 57
Davis, Rosella A. 67
Davis, Sun Ye 50
Dayton, Earl Tresilian 46

Deam, Mary L. 58
Dean, Harry Wilson 65
Decker, Louis 67
De Coito, Louis 49
De Coito, Ann I 45
Decoteau, Joseph 30
Dedegas, Basil 44
Deihl, Edith Jolles 67
Deihl, Renzie Watson 50
De la Costa, Frank A. 52
De la Costa, Jan 32
De la Fuente, Pelegrin 45
De Loffe, John 38
De Martini, Inuise V. 32
Deppermann, Charles 55
Depue, Rodney Albert 29
Detrick, Herbert J. 59
Detrick, Lulu H. 58
Detzer, Linus William 47
DeVries, David Andrew 20
DeVries, Gene 17
DeVries, Gladys L. 45
DeVries, Henry William Sr. 48
DeVries,   Henry William Jr. 14
Dewhirst, Harry Daniel 63
DeWitt, Clyde Alton 65
Dick, Thomas William 71
Dincher, Frederick 30
Dingle, Leila 47
Dingman, Arthur 47
Divine Child, Sister Mary 47
Doig, Leroy Dorry, Jr. 26
Doino, Francis 46
Dominica, Sister M. 45
Dorothy, Sister 40
Dow, William 47
Dowd, Austin 45
Dowling, Richard 38

Downing, Donald Clark 34
Doyle, Emily Norma 343
Doyle, Joseph Desmond 43
Downs, Darley 50
Dragset, Ingie 50
Dreyer, Karl Olaf 59
Drost, Leonard 50
Dudley, Earl C. , Sr. 43
Dudley, Earl C. , Jr. 2
Dudley, Susie Hall 38
Dugas, Alfred Frederick 38
Delaney, Frank Lorraine 56
Dustin, Herbert Warren 30
Dwyre, Allen Louis 39
Dyer, Althea C. 32
Dyer, Harlan L. 34
Dyer, June L. 12
Dyer, Mary 41
Eanswida, Mother M. 26
Earl, George Richard 24
Eaton, Gertrude Mary 52
Eaton, Leon Schultz 60
Ebbesen, Frank E. 51
Eddy, Arthur Louis 65
Edwards, Benjamin Franklin 26
Edwards, Herbert Kenneth 30
Edwards, John 57
Edwards, Mary Constance 24
Eison, George Simon 51
Ekstrand, Martin Eugene 38
Eldridge, Lawrence 6
Eldridge, Norma 8
Eldridge, Paul H. 30
Eldridge, Retha 33
Eleanor, Sister Frances 42
Elizabeth, Sister M. 54
Elliott, Francis Roy 44
Ellis, Adele Marie 24

Elstner, Josephine Elmer 35
Elwood, Joseph Donald 37
Emerson, Ause 65
Epes, Branch Jones Sr. 66
Epes, Branch Jones Jr. 23
Epes, William Fitzgerald 21
Erdman, Joseph James 38
Erickson, Eric Oscar 62
Erickson, Harry Eric 36
Evans, Bertha Rae 40
Evory, Harold William 50
Ewing, Margaret Greenfield 32
Ewing, Roy Emerson 33
Fairweather, Barbara Hayne 28
Fasy, Carroll 44
Fawcett, Alfred Edward Sr. 47
Fawcett, Alfred Jr. 25
Feely, Gertrude 40
Felicidade, M. Mary 47
Felix, Harold (Raphael) 52
Fernandez, Carmen Mary 21
Fernandez, Gregoria 31
Fernandez, Joaquin Jose 25
Fernandez, Juanina Mary 19
Fernandez, Mary Louise 15
Ferrier, John William 34
Ferrier, Theresa Diana 33
Fidelis, Sister M. 36
Fielding, Ralph 35
Fisher, Arthur George 55
Fisher, Frederick Russell 42
Fisher, Ruth Lincoln 36
Fishman, Alvin William 27
Fittinghoff, Nicholas Alexander 40
Fleisher, Henry 37
Fleming, Joseph Lamar 50
Fletcher, Charles Falkner 55
Flint, Alvin Lovett 49

Flint, Sarah Viola 35
Florence, Paul Billington 26
Flores, Joe Tatani 37
Florez, Juanita R. 13
Florez, Julietta Lee 10
Florez, Ramona Samilpa 58
Fluemer, Arnold William 59
Fonger, Leith Cox 48
Fonger, William Henry 53
Ford, Charles Emery 21
Ford, Henry Tagros 14
Ford, William Munroe 22
Forney, William Thomas 33
Fowler, Ernest A. 58
Fox, Frank Christopher 66
Fox, Henry 32
Fox, James Joseph 43
Fox, James Roy 44
Fox, Mattea 24
Fox, Vincent Altizo 28
Francisco, Louis Joseph 23
Frantz, Daniel David 26
Fraser, Elvie 66
Frederica, Sister M. 52
Fredenert, M. M. 31
Freeman, Edward Francis 27
Freeman, Frances Mary 27
Freeman, Jo Fisher 42
Fricke, Herman Henry 61
Fricke, Dorothy 50
Friedl, Joseph 56
Fuller, Sumner Bacon 35
Gabrielson, Carl William 40
Game, Albert A. 93
Gaillard, John Gourdin 56
Galassi, Dominico 50
Gallaher, Robert Franklin 67
Gallagher, Harry Joseph 43

Gallapaue, William Earl 51
Gallit, Henry Emil 41
Galway, Howard 52
Gardiner, Clifford A. 54
Gardiner Elizabeth A. 21
Gardiner, William A. 19
Gardner, Claude Dennis 48
Garmezy, Samuel 52
Garrett, Elwood Llewellin 39
Garrigues, Dwight N. 63
Gavigan, Tripp G. 38
Genevieve, Sister Rose 41
Georgia, Sister M. 46
Gesemyer, Arthur K. 26
Gesemyer, George C. Sr. 50
Gesemyer, George C. Jr. 24
Gewald, Myrtle F. 46
Gibson, Alvin Harvey 35
Giles, Vinton Sela 54
Gilfoil, Katherine 13
Gilfoil, Katherine N. 40
Gilfoil, Lydia Alice 2
Gilfoil, Mary Louise 10
Gilfoil, Patricia Ann 8
Gilfoil, William Scott 35
Girard, Edward 60
Giucondiana, M. M. 26
Gisel, Eugene 45
Gladys, Sister M. 33
Glunz, Charles 69
Glunz, Henrietta H. 65
Godfrey, M. M. 36
Goebel, Otto John 51
Goldman, Edmund 38
Golucke, Louis Harold 56
Goodwin, Martin Luther 51
Gordenker, Alexander 62
Gordon, John J. 71

Gorzelanski, Helen Clara 34

Gotthold, Diana 36

Grady, Virginia H. 24

Gray, Bernice Louise 31

Gray, Edward James 35

Gray, George 32

Grau, Albert 30

Graves, Arthur 57

Greer, Henry 41

Griffn, Elizabeth G. 54

Griffn, Frank 72

Grishkevich, Vitaly Ippolit 52

Grode, Leo 39

Gross, Morton Robert 36

Guicheteau, Armand J. 38

Gunder, Jack H. 24

Gunnels, Robert Lee 41

Guthrie, Mary J. 38

Guthrie, Richard S. 13

Guthrie, Romelda A. 7

Guthrie, William E. 37

Haberer, Emanuel Julius 67

Hacker, Leonard 30

Hackett, Alice 23

Hackett, John Alexander 36

Hageman, Marshall N. 32

Hale, J. Willis 42

Hale, Velma M. 40

Haley, Arthur Edward 53

Haley, James 63

Hall, Norman Shannon 24

Hallett, John Bartlett 63

Ham, Hugh Mack 45

Hammill, Dena M. 29

Hammill, Richard L. 30

Hammill, Rogers N. 4

Hammond, L. D. Lloyd 39

Hamra, Adeeb Joseph 33

Hancock, Lawrence Kelly 29

Hancock, Mary Edna 26

Hannings, Richard Edward 40

Hanson, Donie Taylor 44

Hanson, Rolf Hinnen 37

Hard, Herbert William 38

Hard, Marie Lucille 29

Hardy, Beverly Earl 35

Harms, Lloyd Frederick 51

Harper, Anita Mae 6

Harper, Arthur Edward 26

Harper, Betty Jane 3

Harper, James Albert 28

Harper, Steven Phillip 22

Harrah, Orville 45

Harrah, Rose Marie 44

Harrell, Richard Maxted 32

Harrington, Mary Rose 31

Harris, William S. 30

Harrison, Phillip Francis 46

Harshman, Albert N. 33

Harshman, Anita Wichman 29

Hart, Herbert Henry 28

Hart, Joseph Chittendon 29

Hartnett, Ernest 39

Hatcher, Benjamin Carlile 43

Hause, Charles David 42

Hausman, Louis Michael 55

Haven, Lewis Quincy Jr. 29

Haven, Charlotte Kingsbury(nee Lee)26

Hayme, Carl 63

Haynes, Albert 57

Headley, Donald Grant 54

Healy, Gerald 26

Healy, John 28

Heath, George Eddy 69

Hebard, William Lawrence 32

Heery, Joseph Marion 79

Heesch, Henry John 39

Heichert, Murray Baker 47

Hell, Jan Howard 36

Hellis, Herbert Dean 41

Henderson, Barclay C. 31

Henderson, Dorothy Gardiner 26

Henderson, George William 50

Hendrix, Daisy 41

Hennel, Charles 25

Hennesen, Maria Alexandrina 35

Hennesen, Paul 41

Herndon, Alice Patterson 56

Herndon, Rees Frazer 38

Hertz, Harold Emerson 40

Hess, Arlene F. 11

Hess, Hudson S. 9

Hess, Lois Ellen 5

Hess, R. Bruce 7

Hess, Robert R. 41

Hess, Victor Glen 1

Hess, Viola Ruth 40

Hibbard, James F. 74

Hicks, John Thomas 28

Highsmith, Jerome 71

Hight, Allen H. 48

Hiland, George S. 68

Hildabrand, Carl 55

Hileman, Arthur Daniel 64

Hill, Alva J. 63

Hill, Jay Ward 19

Hill, John 17

Hill, Martha M. 50

Hill, Samuel W. 14

Hinck, Dorothy A. 45

Hinck, Edward M. 19

Hinck, John A. Jr. 15

Hinck, Mary L. 10

Hinck, Robert 13

Hindberg, Walter 40

Hinkley, Jay Augustus 25

Hinkley, Luckey Kathlyn(nee Charter)

Hinsche, Otto 51

Hobson, Henry 41

Hochreiter, Charles J. 51

Hodge, Julia M.74

Hodges, Catherine Taylor 31

Hodges, Harry Mead 32

Hoffmann, Winifred 46

Hogenboom, David Lee 7

Hogenboom, Leonard Samuel 38

Hogenboom, Ruth Groters 37

Hogenboom, Stephen 9

Hokanson, Marie Corp 25

Hokanson, Mons 30

Holt, Jack Berger 31

Holt, Truman Slayton 72

Holy Name, Sister M. 53

Honor, Dorothy Y. 5

Honor, Herbert C. 44

Honor, Herbert Jr. 9

Honor, Vera O. 40

Hood, Thomas Dewitt 45

Hook, Emil V. 64

Horgan, Gregory 30

Hornbostel, Johanna Mario 21

Horton, Frank 63

Hoskins, Colin Macrae 53

Hoyt, Jackson Leach 38

Hubbard, Charles R. 42

Hubbard, Christine 43

Hubbard, William Augustus 66

Hudson, Clay Menafee 65

Hudson, Lewis Clifton 38

Hudson, Primitiva Bertumen 25

Hughes, Harry Bloomfield 61

Hughes, Hugh John 40

Hughes, Russell 38
Hughes, Samuel Alexander 40
Hull, Edwin Miles 55
Hunt, Darcy Swain 37
Hunt, Phray O. 58
Hunter, John Jacobs 38
Hyland, Walter 43
Harpst, Earl Michael 13
Iddings, Paul Loren 44
Immaculate Concepcion, S. R. M. 36
Innis, Charles 3
Innis, David 40
Innis, David James 14
Innis, Donald 12
Innis, Frances 38
Innis, Joseph 6
Irvin, Tom B. 41
Irvine, Bessie 42
Irwin, Henry 52
Isabel, Sister M. 50
Jackson, Myrtle 37
Jacobs, Louis Welch 50
Jacobson, David 66
James, Elizabeth 24
Jamieson, William 63
Janda, Marie Wagner 29
Janda, Robert Lee 38
Jarlath, M. M. of S. T. 39
John, Rees Hopkin 59
Johnson, Cherokee Chickasaw 21
Johnson, Frederick Arnold 36
Johnson, Henry S.15
Johnson, Ralph Murdoch 64
Johnson, Seneca O. 20
Johnson, Thomas W. 10
Johnson, Walter 40
Johnston, Doris 31
Johnston, William W. 33

Jones, Andy 50
Jones, Bernard Edwin 35
Jones, Charles Ernest 68
Jones, Elvis Everett 37
Jones, Ethel L. 46
Jones, Frank Dehaven 60
Jones, Muriel Gertrude 49
Jones, Robert Berian 27
Jones, William Henry 47
Jordon, Thomas Mark 47
Julian, Frederick 32
Juravel, Carl 32
Jurgenssen, August John 47
Jurgenssen, Jennie Grace 50
Justin, Sister M. 51
Kahler, Stannie Daniel 64
Kalkowsky, Adam Edward 37
Kapes, David 42
Katz, Anne 36
Katz, Frances Valerie 17
Katz, Isabella 57
Katz, William Allen 68
Kahn, Maurice 64
Kaminski, Nicodemus 67
Kavanagh, Joseph 29
Kay, Joseph Kerop 63
Kailen, Ernest 25
Kelley, Daniel James 29
Kelly, Harold Maxwell 51
Kemery, Mona Mae 32
Kemp, Oley C. 64
Kern, Helen 27
Kerr, Joseph 40
Ketchum, Gladys Esperanza 33
Keys, Harold Harte 57
Keys, John Dewitt 43
Kidder, Lucia Booth 31
Kidder, Stanley Rast 34

Kiene, Clarence Kirk 36
Kiene, Mildred Evelyn 37
Kienle, Alfred 53
Kilkenny, Edward Michael 39
King, Carl Philip 55
King, Josephine Cook 20
King, Mary Barbara 3
Kingsbury, Stanley Carlos 56
Kinn, Leo 42
Kinney, John Thomas 58
Kinsella, John Sylvester 44
Kitzmiller, Blaine John 24
Kitzmiller, Owen 27
Kleinpell, Robert Mensson 39
Klippert, Edward 31
Knaesche, Herman 53
Knowles, Sambuel Etnyre 48
Koestner, Alfred U. S. 32
Kolodziej, Antonio 58
Kramer, Amelia 34
Kramer, Donald 10
Kramer, Effe 3
Kramer, Georgette 19
Kramer, Harry 63
Knutson, Gilman Darrell 25
Koons, Harry Montford 30
Koons, Thelma Donnelly 28
Krause, William Owen 35
Kringle, Harry 58
Kuhlman, William Henry 65
Kundert, Paul Denton 27
Lacey, Betty 26
Lacey, Kristin 1
Lacey, Sharon 2
Lacey, William Edward 26
Lacy, Merrill Ghent 38
LaFouge, Edward Rudolph 32
Lam, Bo Ming 39

Lamb, William Lee 68
Lambert, Frederick Dankilla 39
Landis, Audrey Blanche 36
Landis, Frederick 6
Landis, Patricia A. 9
Landis, Richard 8
Landis, Roderic 34
LaPointe, William F. 65
LaPorte, Margaret 43
LaPorte, Otto 49
Lappin, Leslie Everett 35
Lauriat, Frederick 44
Lautzenheiser, Ora Ezra 65
LaVigne, Ernest Henri 32
Lawry, Gordon Langford 27
Lawton, Betty Estelle 25
Lawyer, Jerome 31
Leary, John (Jack) Thomas 39
Leary, Paul 25
Lederman, Daniel Bishop 63
Lee, Charlotte Kingsbury 26
Lee, C. W. 51
Lee, David 2
Lee, Elfred M. 3
Lee, Fred M. 45
Lee, James Milton 31
Lee, Margurite 31
LeForge, Roxy 55
Leighton, Ethel Packard 54
Leisring, Lawrence 47
Leitch, James Elmer 51
Leland, James Arthur 41
Leland, Rosamond Cooper 43
Leland, Shirley Mae 4
Leonarda, Sister M. 42
Lesage, Alphons Gerard 40
Lessner, Eva 45
Lessner, Hilda 25

Levy, Ruben 51
Lew, Wah Sun 31
Liggett, James Paul 52
Liles, Lawrence Poland 41
Limpert, John William 56
Lind, Niles John 63
Linn, Harold Adolphus 44
Lochboehler, Bernard 38
Logan, George Lafayette 69
Lombard, Harold Webster 58
Lombard, James Dino 15
Lord, Montague 62
Louis, George James 27
Lovell, Glenn Howard 35
Lovell, Ruth Patterson 35
Lowry, William Arthur 47
Lubarsky, Saul 58
Lucy, Sister Mary 48
Lundquist, Carl Axel 62
Luckman, Elsie Marion 41
Lyon, Herbert 64
McAfee, Clauda 56
McAfee, Leo Gay 50
McAfee, Robert 18
McAllister, Margaret 54
McAnlis, David 13
McAnlis, Jean15
McAnlis, Josephine 50
McAnlis, Ruth 17
McAnlis, William 50
McBride, John Henry 53
McCaffray, Arthur 68
McCalister, Jacob 67
McCandlish, William Foster 44
McCann, James 38
McCarter, Edward Lee 48
McCarthy, Floyd Arthur 45
McCarthy, Marian Florence 30

McCarthy, William Ransom 47
McCarty, Leroy 62
McCarty, Edward Charles 55
McCloskey, Robert E. 30
McClure, Carl Hamlin 28
McClure, Ryanna 25
McCoy, May 63
McCoy, Oscar Gervius 35
McCoy, Mildred Aileen(nee Palmer)27
McCoy, Lois Kathleen 3 days
McCune, Joseph Gerhardt 38
McDonough, Charles A. 65
McEntee, Samuel Sanders 69
McGaretty, Howard Carson 29
McGovern, Lee 40
McGrath, Peter William 25
McGrew, Kinsie 57
McGuiness, Joseph 28
McGuire, Grace Ann 55
McHugh, Patricia Willis 32
McIntosh, Melville Ethelbert 40
McKay, Jean 34
McKee, Robert 31
McKeown, Hugh Michael 48
McLey, Harold J. G. 54
McMann, Frank Patrick 65
McMann, James 27
McMann, John 33
McManus, Ambrose 38
McMullen, Joseph 63
McNamara, Francis Robert 40
McNicholas, John 38
McSorley, Richard 29
McStay, John 64
McStay, John Curry 18
McVey, Bunnie Cecilia 2
McVey, Charles David 34
McVey, Grace Alice Mary 4

McVey, Mary Cecilia 23
Mabry, Frank M. 38
Mabry, Opal Marie 28
MacDonald, Alyse Louise 38
MacDonald, Bob 19
MacDonald, George 13
MacDonald, Helen 17
MacDonald, John 16
MacDonald, Kenneth 63
MacDonald, Margaret 45
MacIntosh, James 80
MacKinnon, James Bowie 30
MacLaren, Donald Ross 41
Madigan, Francis 27
Madsen, Elmer 63
MaGee, George Lyman 53
MaGee, Mary Elizabeth Sr. 56
MaGee, Mary Elizabeth Jr. 22
MaGee, Philip Donald 17
Magill, Charles Newton 68
Mahoney, John Joseph 52
Makepeace, Lloyd Brenecke 31
Malmstrom, Charles Clarence 67
Mangels, Franz 21
Mangels, Henry Ahrends 25
Mangels, John F. 64
Mangels, Margaretta Hermine 22
Mangels, Nieves 28
Mangels, Nieves Chofra 47
Mankin, James Percy 65
Manser, Daniel Leonard 39
Marcella, Sister M. 42
Margerita, Sister M. 33
Margulies, Ruben 32
Marion, Sister Cecilia 39
Marsden, Ralph Walter 23
Martin, Clarence 26
Martin, D. P. 50

Martin, Edgar 34
Massey, Charlotte 65
Masson, Philip 25
Matthew, Sister Rose 29
Matthews, William Jerome 78
Maura, Sister Bernadette 32
Maurashon, Sister 36
Maxcy, Joseph 30
Maxey, Wilburn 64
Maxwell, William Allen 29
Mayer, Harry O'Brien 30
Meagher, Bernard Joseph 36
Meagher, Zora Simmons 36
Mee, Louis 54
Meinhardt, Ruth 33
Melton, Jesse Edgar 56
Merrill, Robert Heath 33
Merritt, Isaac Erwin 73
Messinger, George Marion 32
Metz, Carmen Adoracion 42
Meukow, Coleman Arian 43
Meukow, George Osakina 9
Meukow, Nina Ruth 30
Meukow, Walter Trendel 11
Meyer, Gus Henry 46
Miles, Daniel Walter 27
Miles, Prentice Melvin 40
Miller, Charles Henry 69
Miller, Dorothy Veronica 37
Miller, Gilbert Charles 31
Miller, Helen 29
Miller, John Joseph 22
Miller, Maxine Margaret 28
Mills, John Andrew 28
Millward, Samuel James Jr. 26
Miravalle, Andrew Nino 29
Miriam, Sister Agnes 48
Miriam, Sister Louise 32

Miriam, Sister Thomas 33
Missmer, George Washington 65
Missler, Carl Edward 28
Mitchell, John 68
Mitchell, Thomas 29
Mitchell, William Thomas 22
Moak, Conway Columbus 60
Mock, Charles Gordon 36
Mock, Louise Charmian
          (nee Boomer)28
Mollart, Stanley Vincent 42
Monaghan, Forbes 36
Montesa, Anthony Joseph 20
Montesa, Edward William 17
Montesa, Henrietta F.42
Montesa, John Phillip 19
Montgomery, Antonia Cantilo 23
Montgomery, Ethel Denise 23
Montgomery, Everett Verden 57
Montgomery, Fern Asunsano 35
Moore, Charles F. 15
Moore, Emma G. 50
Moore, George 52
Moore, Joseph Oliver 16
Moore, Joseph W. 52
Moore, Leonard C. 70
Moore, Mae Dancy 59
Moore, Patricia E. 9
Mora, Ernest Joseph 59
Mora, George Castro 19
Mora, Iberia Ortuno 40
Moran, Lawrence Richard 52
Morehouse, Francis B. 58
Morehouse, Phyllis Brenda 23
Morehouse, Winifred Louis 61
Morison, Walter Durrell 37
Morning, John 62
Morris, Leroy 63

Morrision, Carson C. 42
Morrision, Helena V. 35
Mortlock, Frank Oliver 33
Moss, George Herbert 36
Mudd, Maurice 53
Mueller, William Fred 65
Muldoon, Anthony Gregory37
Mulry, Joseph 55
Mulryan, Alma Steiger 43
Mulryan, James Raymond 51
Munger, Henry Weston 67
Munger, Louralee Patrick 66
Murphin, William 53
Murphy, John Joseph 65
Murray, William Elmer 38
Myers, Kenneth Robert 20
Myers, William Tyner 62
Naftaly, Lillian Saidee 50
Naftaly, Nancy Nataly 32
Naido, Joseph 25
Naido, Ruth Louise 37
Nance, Dana Wilson 40
Nash, Gale Blackmarr 5
Nash, Grace Chapman 34
Nash, Ralph 43
Nash, Ralph Stanley 6
Nash, Roy Leslie 1
Nash, Margaret Alice 32
Nathanson, Nathaniel Arthur 44
Nau, Catherine Ludwina 46
Neal, James 54
Neal, Pauline 30
Neibert, Alice Julia 22
Neibert, Henry Edward 70
Neikam, William L. 38
Nelson, Thomas Page 25
Nelson, Valley 55
Newcomb, Walter Cattell 32

Newgord, Julius Gerard 33
Nicholas, John Middleton 43
Nichols, John Randolph 32
Nichols, Leonard David 30
Nicholson, John 27
Nicholson, William 28
Nicol, Celeste Claire 17
Nicol, Charles Bertram 8
Nicol, Fedora Mary 37
Nicol, Jacqueline Winifred 12
Nicol, Normal Arthur 14
Nicoll, David 60
Nicholson, James Francis 54
Nokes, Wilbur Charles 39
Norton, Alfred 32
Nuger, Isaac 31
Nuttall, Edmond 45
O'Boirne, Vincent 45
O'Brien, John Robert 30
O'Brien, Michael Wilbur 33
Obst, Thomas James 28
O'Conner, Clarence 57
Ode, Carsten Linnevold 37
O'Hara, Kathleen F. 1
O'Hara, Lorraine Betty 22
O'Hara, Michael Joseph 24
O'Hara, Michael Joseph Jr. 1 month
O'Haver, Goldie Aimee 41
Ogan, William Clarence 66
Olivette, Sister M. 37
Olsen, Lillian Agnes 36
O'Malloy, John Bryan 30
O'Neill, James 53
Oppenheimer, John 38
Osbon, Bert Paul 60
O'Shaughnessy, Martin 55
Oss, Norman Alfred Jr. 19
O'Toole, John Patrick 41

Overton, Elbert Monroe 32
Owens, Hoyle Williams 51
Pacheco, Michael Angelo 43
Paget, Cyrus 57
Paige, Eldene Elinor 31
Palmatier, Ellery Leroy 32
Palmer, Clarence Hugh 44
Palmer, Mildred Ailene 27
Pangborn, Wallace 41
Parham, Archer Brandon 55
Parker, Bertha F. 44
Parker, Bertha Helena 54
Parker, Helen Dorothy 41
Parker, Roy Lester 52
Parker, Wilbur Clarke 56
Parquette, William Stewart 29
Parish, Edward John Jr. 33
Passmore, Fred J. 40
Patricia, Sister M. 60
Patricia, Sister Marie 37
Patterson, Myron 49
Pauli, Ralph 56
Pawley, Charles Thomas 29
Pearson, Cecil Leroy 51
Peck, Lawrence Leroy 41
Peek, Elvin Roland 54
Penny, Harold Ray 30
Pepper, Charles John 48
Perfecta, Sister 41
Perkins, Willie Ray 29
Pearlman, Max O. 49
Perry, Walter Lee Gihon 73
Pflug, Emma 33
Phillips, Eleanor Marie 27
Phillips, Howard Lester Sr. 30
Phillips, Howard Lester Jr. 3
Philp, Dorothy Suzanne 38
Pickell, William H. 63

Pickens, Henri B. 35
Pickering, Camille Elaine 58
Pickering, John Kuykendall 58
Pierce, Margaret Helen 29
Pirassoli, Charles William 48
Pitcher, Susie Josephine 43
Plowman, Claire Elizabeth 1
Plowman, Elizabeth Oxford 32
Plowman, George Harden 29
Pohl, Gordon Robert 30
Pollard, Harriet Emma 64
Pond, Helen 54
Porter, Lloyd Thomas 66
Posner, Irving 58
Precino, Thomas 72
Preiser, Rosa Christian 51
Preston, Rose Marie 37
Price, Walter Scott 67
Priestner, Joseph 41
Purnell, John Ferguson 37
Purnell, Lillian Gottrell 24
Putney, Harry Bryan 44
Quillinan, Frank William 37
Quinn, Grant 33
Raleigh, Daniel Mead 36
Rand, Grace 56
Rast, Beni 50
Ratcliffe, Jesse Walker 60
Raymond, Mona 48
Reardon, Francis 46
Redard, Alexander James 63
Redempta, Sister M. 42
Reich, Bertha Harris 43
Reid, William Robert 34
Reilly, Matthew 44
Reinhart, James H. 33
Reith, Joseph 50
Repetti, William 60

Repikoff, John 49
Reuter, James 28
Rey, Sister Maria del 36
Reynolds, Ralph 38
Rhudie, Ada Woodsworth 56
Rhudie, Oscar Peter 57
Rice, Williard Lamont 50
Richards, Edwin Franklin 54
Richards, Mary Fielding 35
Riddle, Henry Hampton 51
Rider, Frank Jackson 50
Riffel, Dorothy Ann 13
Riffel, Esther N. 42
Riffel, Gordon William 14
Riffel, Retta Leona 16
Riffel, William E. 45
Riley, Charles 25
Rively, William 26
Rivers, William Richard 31
Rizzuti, Oarm 36
Robert Marie, Sister 32
Roberts, Elizabeth 60
Roberts, Galien Sofia 22
Roberts, Odin Gregory 56
Robertson, Joseph H. 59
Robie, Merle Steel 25
Robinson, Charles A. 32
Robinson, Graham Post 25
Robinson, Leslie D. 57
Robinson, Roberta May 33
Rodgers, Frances 51
Roebuck, Brooks Waldo 46
Roebuck, May Ephrom 33
Roehr, Oscar Carl 47
Roehr, Pauline Marie 45
Roeper, Ludwig Earl 43
Rohrbaugh, Olive 64
Rohrer, Helen Brian 44

Rohrer, Samuel Lewis 39
Rosabella, Sister 41
Roscom, Jerry Nicholas 63
Rose, Sister Catherine 28
Rose Jude, Sister 28
Rose Marie, Sister 37
Rosella, Sister 46
Rosenthal, Leon 73
Rosier, Warren 33
Ross, Ervin Clinton 56
Ross, George 31
Ross, Gladys Mary 51
Ross, Lillian 43
Routhier, George Silvio 30
Rowland, M. Elston 49
Ruane, John 24
Runyon, Richard Earl 27
Rurka, Steve 25
Russell, Aida B. 22
Russell, Diana Marie 2
Russell, Earl Edwin 47
Russell, Theresa White 41
Ryall, Theodore Lee Jr. 20
Rydberg, Carl Gunnar 38
Safino, Esther A. 35
Sager, Frederick James 35
Salamy, Abraham George 26
Salet, Elizabeth Ann 24
Salter, Russell 33
Samara, Edward Thomas 30
Samara, Saleem George 65
Sams, Gerald R. 33
Sampson, James Stewart 62
Sanborn, Donald George 39
Sanders, Albert J. 43
Sanders, David J. 7
Sanders, Edna F. 44
Sanders, Florence Smith 47

Sanders, Phillip Herman 40
Sands, Martin Paul 44
Sands, Mildred Marie 40
Satterfield, Frederick Malone 45
Saunders, Emma 53
Saunders, Frank Sr. 55
Saunders, Frank Jr. 12
Saunders, Norma Louise 17
Sayre, Bruce 53
Scaff, Alvin Hewitt 29
Scaff, Lawrence A. 2
Scaff, Mary Lee 28
Scarlett, Jane Agnes 61
Scarlett, William John 62
Schechter, Seymour 35
Scheidl, Rudolph John 30
Scherer, Doris 35
Scherer, Morris C. 32
Scherer, Richard 1
Schermerhorn, William H. 73
Scheuermann, Dennis Friday 1
Scheuermann, Gustav John 31
Scheuermann, Gwendolyn Marta 4
Scheuermann, Helen Friday 28
Schier, Kathleen Grant 34
Schier, Samuel Saunders 46
Schmidt, Richard Joseph 27
Scholastica, Sister M. 40
Schoppe, Leonard Albert 73
Schoppe, Lillian A. 71
Schroeder, Louis 56
Schorth, Max Brune 69
Schubert, Edward C. 66
Schuster, Helene Rothmeister 48
Schuster, Helene Jeanete 25
Schuster, John Howard 50
Schworer, Donald Valentine 28
Scofield, Donald Eugene 63

Scott, Elizabeth Steele 25
Scott, Joe Edwin 37
Scott, Lyle Cecil 41
Seals, Margaret Mildred 40
Sechrist, David P. 7
Sechrist, Harold 33
Sechrist, John W. 2
Sechrist, Marguerite 30
Shaffer, William Robert 25
Shapiro, Herman 45
Shaw, Herbert Wesley 48
Shaw, Kate Sibley 64
Shaw, Walter Ray 57
Sherk, David Robert 5
Sherk, Gerry Ann 1
Sherk, Margaret Coulson 27
Shimmel, Edith 52
Shoemaker, Abbott Paul 45
Shropshire, Harry Wesley 23
Shurdut, Joseph Moses 48
Siena, Sister M. 43
Silen, Elizabeth Jean 19
Silen, Joan Bradford 10
Silen, Margaret Elizabeth 44
Silen, Shirley Ann 17
Silloway, Merle 47
Simatovich, Nicholas Joseph 34
Simmons, Ernest Edgeworth 36
Sklenar, Anthony Joseph 33
Small, Elizabeth Studavant 51
Small, Frank Sylvester 51
Small, Helen Elizabeth 18
Smallwood, Robert 36
Smith, Alfred Whitacre 32
Smith, B. Ward 55
Smith, Dewey Woods 46
Smith, Harry Josselyn 74
Smith, Harry Thurston 45

Smith, Joseph John 42
Smith, Paul L. 19
Smith, Stephen L. 50
Smith, Viola R. 52
Smith, Willard Horace 42
Smoyer, Egbert M. 54
Snead, Elizabeth B. 23
Snead, Mary Carol 3
Snead, Paul Kindig 29
Snead, Paul Laurence 4
Sniffen, Genevieve Marie 30
Sniffen, John Mark 38
Snyder, Gaines 33
Snyder, Mary Lucille 33
Snyder, William Raymond 41
Soares, John Stanislas 64
Sottile, Frank Joseph 57
Spatz, Oswald 55
Spear, Earl Franklin 46
Spencer, William Meek 34
Spencer, William Robert 44
Sperry, Henry M. 38
Stacy, Gertrude Rosie 23
Stahl, Alfred Joaquin 63
Stancliff, Leo 31
Stark, Clarence Theo 52
Starr, John Bernal 47
Stearns, Mary Jean Stephens 40
Steffens, Raymond Harold 45
Steven, Oswald Barnard 51
Stevens, Leslie Eugene 55
Steward, Basilia Torres 31
Stewart, John Norman 38
Still, Dorothy 30
Stiver, Edna Theresa 56
Stiver, Joseph Alfred 62
Stocking, Charles Samuel 64
Stokes, Henry Milton 37

Stoll, Eugene Leo 40
Stoneburner, Edna 37
Strong, James Walter 69
St. Thomas, Federico Jr. 27
Stuart, David Lennox 32
Stubo, Knutty Christian 52
Stumbo, John David 57
Stump, Irene J. 41
Stump, Lawrence 46
Stumpf, William Jerome Jr. 29
Sturm, Stanley Marcellus 49
Sudhoff, Raymond George 23
Sullivan, Edward 28
Sullivan, Russell 49
Suro, Reuben 30
Swanson, Ruth Pauline 51
Sykora, Frank 47
Tabor, John 66
Tapia, Edwin Joseph Jones 27
Taylor, William Leonard 16
Taylor, Willis L. 35
Tekippe, Owen 36
Terrill, Thomas Star 32
Terry, Albert Henry 39
Terry, Carol Louise 31
Terry, Joseph Edward 29
Teurnee, Maurice Conrad 39
Theophila, Sister M. 36
Theudere, M. Mary of S. P. 36
Thomas, Antonita B. 24
Thomas, Dollie Mae 2
Thomas, Elizabeth Francisco 9 days
Thomas, Florence A. 3
Thomas, Howard Wilton 29
Thomas, Robert Lee 22
Thompson, David Bill 37
Thompson, Floyd Addison 57
Thompson, Leslie Daniel 60

Tinling, Don 54
Titlow, Marian Phillips 32
Todd, Carrie Edwina 33
Todd, George Jr. 35
Todd, Noel 34
Todebush, Ralph Bernard 43
Tootle, Mildred Caroline 24
Torkeson, Edward 67
Treubig, John F. 47
Tribble, Jesse Lee 25
Trogstad, Martha Bowler 29
Tuck, Ernest E. 55
Tuck, Helen G. 55
Tuite, Thomas 38
Tulloch, James Garfield Jr. 36
Tulloch, William James 1
Tutten, Daniel Eugene 44
Ullman, Frank 46
Ullman, Tamara Alexis 43
Urquhardt, Edward J. 61
Urquhardt, Maud J. 55
Urquhardt, Stanley P. 15
Vandenplas, Pierre Gaston 51
Vanderburg, Charles Osborn 56
Vernick, Joseph Barry 31
Vicroy, Sigle Allen 68
Villar, Charles Herman 34
Vincent, Louis Lester 61
Vitalis, Sister Mary 53
Vogelgesang, John 29
Von Hess, Jack C. 24
Voss, William Frederick 63
Vinson, Olivert Castille 30
Vinson, Thomas Chalmers 30
Wagelie, Cunval Andreas 58
Wagner, John Robert 55
Wagner, Rudolph 53
Wahlgreen, Beulah King 38

Walker, Alfred Francis 42

Walker, Harold 63

Walker, Orian Love 55

Wallace, Frank Byron 46

Waples, James Francis 41

Ward, William Vines 32

Wareham, Johnson Matthew 35

Warner, Carl 46

Warner, Mary Delilah 61

Warren, Fred Prince 67

Warren, Harry Pre 63

Waterstradt, Albert Edward 33

Wathen, John David 31

Webster, Walter Jr. 21

Weems, Alexander Murray 32

Weibel, Mary Eileen 22

Weil, Charles William 72

Welborn, George 61

Welch, Leo 37

Wells, James 55

Wells, Jessie 53

Wenetzki, Charles Eduard 56

West, Glenn Key 38

West, Hester D. 36

Wester, Arthur W. 29

Westmoreland, Graham Bradley 38

Westmoreland, Victoria Maria 22

Wheeler, Hiram Albert L. 9

Wheeler, Ida Ellen 28

Wheeler, Robert Antony 11

Wheeler, Robert J. M. 42

Whitaker, Evelyn Eddy 52

Whitaker, Helen Elizabeth 14

Whitaker, Jocelyn Alfred 54

Whitaker, Margaret Evelyn 18

Whitaker, Septimus Tom B. 52

White, George Henry Jr. 30

White, Nathaniel Walker 40

Whitesides, John Garrett 32

Whitmoyer, George Irwin 49

Wichman, Daniel Lee 2

Wichman, Douglas 1

Wichman, Ernest Hermsen 29

Wichman, Gladys Caroline 23

Widdoes, Alice S. 67

Widdoes, H. W. 71

Wienke, Carl Ludwig 10

Wienke, Carmen Aurora 38

Wienke, Edward Peter 23

Wienke, Elizabeth Carmen 18

Wienke, Frederick Johan 13

Wienke, Marcie Christina 21

Wienke, Theresa Victoria 16

Wienke, Violet Alma 15

Wilcox, Lyle 52

Wilcox, Wendel 16

Wilder, Charlie 54

Wiley, Samuel 25

Williams, Clyde Scott 28

Williams, Gordon L. 35

Williams, Greta R. 38

Williams, Jack 37

Williams, Leona H. 35

Williams, Roy Harold 41

Willmann, George J. 47

Wills, Hugh Clarence 36

Wills, Ida Gertrude 2

Wills, Jane S. 26

Wilson, Anita Marie 1

Wilson, Edward John 49

Wilson, Harold Norman 51

Wilson, James Reese 63

Wilson, Jesse Smith 28

Wilson, Joan Marie (nee Smith)

Wilson, John 66

Wilson, John Brownlee 53

Wilson, Wilbur Scott 80
Winn, Charles Robert 50
Winn, Ethel May 39
Winship, S. Davis 53
Winsor, Christine 25
Wislizenus, Claire Alberton 68
Wittman, Arthur Carl 54
Wolff, Charles 24
Wolfe, Carrie A. 63
Wolfe, Leslie 68
Wolfgram, Ida Mae 31
Wolfgram, Leroy Herbert 39
Wood, Joseph Palmer 46
Woodin, Charles Wesley 34
Woodrooff, William Dickey 66
Woods, Robert Gordon 67
Woodworth, Ruth A. 44
Workman, Doris Therese 14
Workman, George Welman 57
Workman, Helen Marie 23
Workman, Katherine Marie 55
Workman, Lillian Ann 20
Workman, Mildred Josephine 16
Worthen, Helen Margaret 46
Worthen, Thomas Roy 48
Wright, Laurdes Dizon 27
Wright, Randall William 39
Wright, Tobias Henry 66
Yankey, Mary Louise Curran 27
Yankey, William Ross 31
Yarborough, Alta Lenna 33
Yarborough, Henry Edward Jr. 33
Yard, Lester Hollaster 41
Yartz, John 47
Yearsley, Helen Ellison 34
Young, Robert Alexander 28
Young, Roman 69
Young, William H. 40

Zervoulakos, Alfred Gregory 21
Zigler, William McKinley 46
Zillig, Martin 62

BRITISH

Aaron, Jean Margaret
Aaron, John David
Aaron, John Maurice
Airiess, Eric Mather
Aitkens, John Reginald
Albine, Sister
Aldred, Herbert
Allen, Constance
Allen, Elizabeth
Allen, Margaret
Allen, Phillip
Anderson, David
Andrews, Nadia
Andrews, Ronald V.
Arnovick, Mary M.
Arnovick, Charles
Arnovick, George M.
Azevedo, Olga
Azevedo, Beatrice
Bairgrie, Alexander
Baigrie, Bertha
Baildon, Aimee
Balfour, William
Balis, David
Balis, Jenny
Barnes, Katherine
Barnes, Kenneth
Barnes, Robert Barnes,
William Frank
Barr, Fiona
Barr, Margaret

Barr, Ronald
Barrett, Cecil
Beck, Arthur Charlesworth
Beebee, Walter Willis
Beeman, Sarah
Behenna, Dorothy
Bennett, Lillian
Bentley, Edward
Birchall, James Richardson
Black, James
Blair, Leslie
Blechynden, Lindsey DeClarke
Boddington, Dorothy
Boddington, Richard John
Bonner, Norman Ellis
Bosch, Edward Henry Brett
Boswell, George James
Bradshaw, John William
Brambles, James Christopher
Brambles, Margaret Lillian
Brambles, Ralph Douglas
Brambles, Elizabeth
Brambles, Grace
Brambles, Patricia
Brambles, Ralph Bramwell,
Edward Kennedy
Bramwell, Helen L.
Breson, Lillian
Brewster, Charles
Brooks, Anna
Brooks, Cyril H.
Brooks, Kenneth S.
Brooks, Leonard C.
Brooks, Rose E.
Buckberrough, Rosa
Buhler, Charles
Burn, Robert
Burn, William Angus

Bush, Edward Stanley
Cameron, John Fraser
Corley, Thomas Ekstrom
Celestine, Sister M.
Chapman, Maurice Bonham
Chong, Charles
Christian, Frederick
Clark, Wallace Robert
Clarke, Esther Millicent
Clarke, Evelyn Victoria
Cohen, Florence Frances
Corfield, Isla
Corfield, Gillian I.
Coxon, Jane Margaret
Crabbe, Kenneth Murray
Creech, Henry
Crewe, James
Curtis, John Shearme
Dalgleish, Mabel Emily
Dalgleish, Mabel Margaret
Da Silva, Augustus
D'Authreau, John Harold
Dickson, Elsa Fanny
Dodd, Gloria Lydia
Dodd, Reginald Morris
Dodd, Zina Andreevna
Dolores, Sister Maria
Donald, William
Dos Remedios, Henry Joseph
Douglas, William
Doull, Agnes
Doull, William
Dow, James Frederick
Drysdale, Thomas Douglas
Duncan, Ian Murray
Dwyer, Thomas
Ethelburga, Sister M.
Fairweather, James Edwin

Falkner, Angeles Martin
Falkner, James Albert
Falkner, Ronald D.
Fitzgerald, Desmond S.
Fox, Catherine Mary
Fox, Christopher Charles
Fox, Charles James
Fox, Lawrence
Fox, Patrick James
Fox, Stephen George
Frampton, Amy Beatrice
Frampton, Muriel
Freckleton, Thomas
Geddes, Eric
Geddes, Jean Frances
Gillett, Bertram John
Gordon, Mary
Gordon, Matthew Dobie
Grant, Helen Gordon
Gray, Irene Betty
Green, Louisa
Green, Michael John
Greenland, Lucy Violet
Griffth, Owen Ambrose
Grimmant, David Henry
Haigh, Annie
Haigh, Jesse
Haigh, Renee Mary
Haigh, Victor Alfred
Hails, Henry Forster
Hallowes, Elsie Mary
Hamblett, James
Hanson, Frank Raymond
Hardcastle, Charles Otterson
Harris, William Francis Geo.
Hayes, Jean
Hayes, Kathleen Elizabeth
Hayes, Michael Aloysius

Haymes, Maxwell Freeland L.
Hearn, Martin Everard
Hill, Rowland George
Hodges, Arthur J.
Hodges, Eleanora
Hoey, Richard C.
Hoey, Rut9+h C.
Hollyer, William George
Horridge, George Redvers
Hughes, Donald Francis
Humphries, John Hugh
Hurley, Patrick
Hutchison, David Dick
Irvine, Jean
Ismail, Sheil Salim
Jackson, James Gregory
Jamieson, Stewart
Jaques, Stanley Heath Jay,
John Leslie
John, Dorothy A.
John, Helen M.
John, Kathleen Elizabeth
John, May
Jones, Henry Victor
Jordon, Kathleen Agnes
Kane, John William James
Kay, Aubony Taylor
Kennedy, Eileen
Kennedy, Erna V.
Kennedy, Kathleen M.
Kennedy, Robert C.
Kennedy, Robert C. Jr.
Kew, Cecil
King, Agnes Isabel
King, Charles Forrester
Kotliar, Betty
Lane Fox, Sister Gertrude
Lee, Ansie

Legg, John Alexander
Leith, Henry Earl
L.eith, Mair
Leith, Rosemary
Leyshon, Frank Howard
Ligertwood, Charles Liddell
Lloyds, Edwin William
McClure, Lawrence Maxton
McGinness, Thomas John
McGregor, Robin
McKerchar, Ian
McLeod, Hugh
McMaster, John Wilson
McMaster, Norah Helen
McWhirter, Hugh Fergus
MacIntyre, Norah Peal 1
MacIntyre, Ronald
MacKay, Kathleen Mary M.
MacLaren, Willia2m Hart
MacLean, Hector James Hilder
MacLean, Margaret
MacWilliam, Jean Cowan Shanks
MacWilliam, Richard Niven
MacWilliam, Scott
Malcolm, Harry Redd
Malpas, William Richard J.
Mann, William Ronald
Mather, William Gladston
Maxima, Sister M.
Medina, Elfrida Elizabeth
Meadows, Gordon
Miller, Charles Walter
Miller, David Carlton
Miller, Patricia Ann
Miller, Robert Walker
Miller, Vera Alexandra
Moore, Calvert Hildabrand
Morley, Howard

Morris, Robert Owen
Morrison, Geoffrey Lionel
Morrison, Robert Alexander
Naismith, William Cunningham
Nathanson, Jean L.
Nathanson, Marie Emsley
Nelson, Archibald Graham
Newgord, Esther
Newsome, Peter Noel Vesey
Nicolson, John
Norton-Smith, Kenneth James
Oliver, Violet Lillian
Palmer, Bertha Lucy
Palmer, John Blything
Palmer, Ronald Singleton
Parker, Herman Vercomb
Parquette, Rosemarie Dorothy
Paterson, James
Paterson, Mary D.
Patey, Walter Bruce
Patricia, M. M.
Pedder, Gerald Herbert
Pedersen, Gwendolyn Florence
Perry, David Henry
Philomena, Sister Marie
Piatnitsky, Olga Pavlovna
Piercy, Arthur
Pollard, Arnold
Pollock, Yvonne Celia
Pope, Harvey Collie
Porter, Robert John
Price, Arthur
Price, Elizabeth Sible
Price, William Samuel
Prismall, Allen
Proudfoot, Alexander
Prout, James Ormand
Quinn, Bernard Alphonsus

213

Redfern, Foster
Reich, Joseph
Reid, George William
Richardson, William Bryan
Robertson, Howard Laird
Roche, Barbara Pavlovna
Roche, Mary Roberta
Rodda, Hababah
Rodgers, Albert G.
Rodgers, Marcus G.
Rodgers, Rosa N.
Royston, John
Rushton, Violet Edith
Rushton, George
Ryde, Sonia
Sawyer, Paula Adelatie
Schelkunoff, Vladimir Peter
Scott, David Alexander
Serephins, Sister Mary of the
Sinclair, Jeffrey Whitfeld
Small, William Valentine
Smith, George Albert
Smith, Joan Marie
Smith, John Alwynne George L.
Smith, Louis
Smith, William A.
Smith, Arthur Linton
Spackman, Harold C.
Spackman, Winifred D.
Steel, James Laurie
Stephens, Sydney
Stratton, Joseph Grant L.
Strong, Martin
Symonds, John
Templer, Angela Mary
Templer, Ann Hazel
Templer, James Robert
Templer, Jennifer S.

Thomson, Elizabeth Marie
Thomson, Robert Allison
Tomkin, Anna Georgvina
Tonkin, Marguerite Janet A.
Tonkin, Mathew McNair
Tonkin, William Charles Geo.
Turner, William
Tyre, Alexander James
Watson, William
Watt, Effe Margaret
Watt, Olive Charlotte
Watty, Lewis Thomas
Webb, Frank Hardy
Whittal, Henry Cecil
Wightman, Arthur John
Wightman, Eglington John
Wightman, Ethelgiva Frances
Wightman, Irene Nellie
Wightman, William Dana
Willder, Katie Agnes
Williams, Hugh Hosking
Williams, John Joseph
Williamson, Margaret
Wilson, Ian Thurburn
Wilson, Walter James
Windle, Wilfred Edwin
Wood, Charles John
Wooding, Wilfred
Wright, Arthur
Wulfildan, M. M.
Yewen, Nina Efgenieva
Zacharias, Hans

AUSTRALIAN

Bargallo, Amelia
Bargallo, Salvadora

Best, Francis
Blanchard, Mary
Byrne, Joseph
Cruice, William
Deane, Patrick
Dougherty, John Hercules
English, Leo
Gygar, Andrew
Holt, Bridget Trist
Holt, Edna May
Hughes, Allen John
Jackson, Gordon
Kemp, Joy Elizabeth
Laycock, William Murray B.
Laycock, Kathleen
McCarthy, Charles
McGuire, Mary Kathleen
MacMaster, John Dunlop
Nield, Frederick Bodin
O'Donnell, Gerard
Pinkerton, Stanley Corey
Pinkerton, Velma
Richards, Thomas Robert
Ridley, John Edwin
Sagor, Amy Lida
Sexton, Francis
Smith, Flora Beryl
Taylor, Betsy. Doris
Taylor, Charles
Thomas, George Frederick
Walsh, Francis

CANADIAN

Abarista, Sister Mary
Alphonse, de Ligori
Angeline, Sister Mary
Ann Celine, Sister Saint
Ann Marie, Sister
Arcand, Ulric
Begin, Joseph
Benoit, Mother Mary of Saint
Bernard, Sister M.
Bleau, Albert
Brouillard, Rodrigue
Charter, Catherine
Charter, Luckey Kathlyn
Charter, Thomas Henry
Christophe, Soeur Saint
Clotilde, Sister M.
Dalmis, Michael
Desmarais, Camille
Everista, Mother
Frician, Sister M.
Gabriel, Sister De-Anuncion
Gabriel, Sister S.
Geofferey, Joseph
Gustav, Sister Saint
Harper, Ella Mae
Hodgson, Francis Xavier
Holloway, Glen Irwin
Humphries, Robert Maxwell
Jarry, Andre
Jepson, Leon Baynes
Joseph de Bethlehem, Sister
Lawton, Herbert
Loptson, Adulsufinn
Magnus Loptson, Faith C.
McCullough, Henry
McKenzie, Catherine
McKenney, Warren Evans
Madeline Marie Barrat, Sister
Marie de Preciux Sang, Sister
Mathiew, Soeur Saint
Maurice, Sister Mary

Mooney, Luke Henry
Murphy, William J.
Nicol, Arthur Louis
Paget, Kathleen M.
Paget, Margaret E. J.
Paget, William H. W.
Palmer, Blanche Evelyn
Philp, George Ansel
Pierre Claver, Sr. S.
Rene, M. M.
Rosemonde, M. M
Shaw, Alice Florence (Beyes)
Victorice, M. M. of Saint
Williams, William C.
Ymer, M. M. de Saint

DUTCH (Netherlands)

Aalten, Hans van
Albana, Sister N.
Alarda, Sister M.
Aldenhuysen, Godfred
Alice, Sister M.
Alphonsa, Sister M.
Anastasia, Sister M.
Bathildis, Sister M.
Bieschop, Roosegaade J. Philip
Blans, Thomas
Blewanus, Gerard
Boggiam, Max
Borght, Francisco van der
Bos, Maria Theresa
Burer, John
Cajetani, Sister M.
Canisia, Sister M.
Coenders, John
Corsten, Andrew

Croonen, Joseph
Decorata, Sister
DeHaan, Isaac
Dekker, John
DeWit, E.
Donata, M.
Dyk, Francisco van
Egonia, Sister M.
Engelen, Felite van
Es, Roelof van
Evangelista, Sister M.
Fransen, Martinus
Gentila, Sister M.
Glansbeek, Reiner van
Groonen, Josef
Groot, Petrus
Hagen, Jan van
Hartog, William
Hendricks, Nicholas Wilhelmus
Houben, Arnold
Intven, Joseph
Janssens, Alberta
Janssens, Marius Cornelus
Jonkerguuw, Hubertus Josephus
Joseph M.
Jurgens, Constans (Bishop)
Keet, Teodoro
Kemperman, Richard
Kilb, Antony
Loo, Cornelio van der
Lutgardis, M.
Magdala, Sister M.
Margretta, Sister M.
Mees, Gregory
Mees, William
Michels, Derk Aw.
Modesta, Sister M.
Notenboom, Jacobus Cornlis

Odyk, Anton van
Oomen, Antonius Paulus
Opstal, Van William
Polycarpa, Sister M.
Raben, Karel Hendrik
Reimers, Christian Hendrik
Reoinjen, Henricus van
Ruyter, Jan
Schaeffer, Johannes Henricus
Slangen, Peter
Sleegers, Henry
Smits, Adrianus
Steyger, Adrianus
Tangelder, Gerardo
Timp, Pedro John
Tonus, Cornelio
Trienekens, Gerardus F.
Van der List, Petrus J.
Van Overveld, Antonio
Van Vlierden, Constant Matthys
Verhoven, Joseph
Vincent, Jacobus
Vlasvelo, Pedro
Vrakking, Johan
Werff, Alice Catherine
Werff, Milagros Herrera
Werff, Pieter Hildebrand
Werff, Wanda Oliva
Werkhoven, Jacobux
Willemina, M.
Willemsen, Bernardus J.
Zegwaard, Francis Henry

NORWEGIAN

Aanonsen, Nels Marion
Abrahamsen, Blarne William

Christensen, Yugvar Kjell
Eilertsen, Thomas
Einarsen, Ruben Helmer
Monsen, Olaf
Oyen, Nils
Pedersen, Erling Bjoern
Petersen, Knut Selmer
Petersen, Trygve

POLISH

Adelski, Borys
Bieniarz, Edward
Gang, Samuel Sam
Hirschorn, Marcus
Keller, Harry
Krzewinski, Ludwig
Lerner, Helen
Lounsbury, Irene Olshenke
Mingelgruen, Wilhelm
Neuman, Rudolph Ham
Propper, Norbert
Rabinowicz, Icko
Rabinowicz, Mordchal
Sackiewicz, Alexander
Sackiewicz, Wladyslaw
Sielski, Wladyslaw
Sielski-Jones, Yadwiga Teresa
Soroka, Samuel Chaim
Strzalkowski, Henry
Szpigielman, Marek
Wahraaftig, Oswald
Werbner, Izydor

George Holt, Jr.

ITALIAN

Bulli, Angelo
Coll-Mellini, Helen
Ghigliotti, Giuseppe
Ghigliotti, Lourdes
Gircognini, Lorenzo
Gircognini, Manuela
Gircognini, Maria Lisa
Gislon, Antonio
Giuseppefranco, Altomonte
Mellini, Rudolph
Vigano, Angelo
Vigano, Camilla
Vigano,   Tuillo
Vigano, Augusto
Vigano, Federico